Uppity Women
of the New World

VICKI LEÓN

LARGE PRINT

Oxford

Copyright © Vicki León

First published by Conari Press

Published in Large Print 2003 by ISIS Publishing Ltd,
7 Centremead, Osney Mead, Oxford OX2 0ES
by arrangement with Conari Press

Leon, Vicki

Library of Cong Uppity women of ublication Data
can be obtai the New World / of Congress
Vicki Leon

315.
4 LP

British Librar 1465275 lication Data
León, Vicki,–
    Uppity women of the New World. –
    Large print ed.
    1. Women – America – History
    2. Women – America – Biography
    3. Women colonists – America – Biography
    4. Women explorers – America – Biography
    5. Large type books
    I. Title
    305.4'09227

ISBN 0–7531–9850–9 (hb)
ISBN 0–7531–9851–7 (pb)

Printed and bound by Antony Rowe, Chippenham

To my own unquenchably uppity women,

With my love and utter admiration:
Valerie Conroy, Mary Lou Davis, and Athena Poysky

Contents

Introduction

As a new arrival on the wild shores of Massachusetts Bay Colony, Puritan poet Anne Bradstreet wrote, "I found a new world, and new manners, at which my heart rose." As you meet the more than 200 redoubtable women in this book, you'll see her use of the phrase "new world" in a fresh light — one that stretches Bradstreet's meaning even further.

Although the centuries between the European Renaissance and the American Civil War usually get stuck with labels like "the Industrial Age" and "the Colonial Period", these defining terms miss the mark. They're too cramped, too Caucasian — and way too male. Beginning in the 1500s, and into the mid-1800s, an astonishing array of women of all colors, countries, and creeds found their own heartlifting "new worlds". Despite efforts to stop them, these Marías and Sallies sallied forth, determined to take the status out of status quo.

These women lived in the age when *global* first became a word. The notion gradually took hold that the world was cluttered with oceans and land masses, and one could even sail around it. In the vanguard were vixens like France's Jeanne Baret, who became the

1

planet's first secret circumnavigator; Spain's Isabel de Guevara, who survived inept planning and the piranha-laden waters of South America to cofound Buenos Aires; England's Mary Haydock, a horse thief condemned to be an early Aussie; and Scotland's Isabelle Gunn, whose love of canoes and nasty weather made her the ultimate Hudson's Bay Company employee in Canada.

While Europeans of every stripe and gender were dashing across oceans, trying to reach dry land before succumbing to scurvy or starvation, native dwellers in these places were getting downright peeved. What with incessant welcome parties for the pale and demanding newcomers, life got way too hectic. Local standouts like Pocahontas and Wetamo in North America, Bartira in South America, Kapiolani in Hawaii, and Mauatea in Tahiti were critical during those first contacts. If it weren't for the food, know-how, road directions, and personal friendships offered by indigenous women, none of the putative explorers or colonizers, from Cortés to the Mayflower Gang, would have survived to make the history books.

Right off the bat, whether as new arrivals or as part of the welcoming party, women began racking up firsts. Among the superlatives: saintly Rose of Lima, the first woman of color to achieve Catholic superstardom; slave Mary Johnson, who in 1622 became the first free black in the United States; and English writer-networker Mary Montagu, who brought back a dandy souvenir from her travels — the first workable method of smallpox vaccination used in the West.

Women sought new frontiers in other ways, too. Venturesome balloonists on both sides of the Atlantic, from Marie Blanchard to Madame Delon, broke the bounds of Earth — sometimes with a bigger bang than expected. There were inventively spiritual leaders like Jemima Wilkinson, a "second messiah" who created her own Eden in upstate New York. Game dames didn't hesitate to take crime to new heights, either. Smooth counterfeiter Mary Butterworth created a cottage industry, making rogue money in Rhode Island. Anne Bonney and Mary Read, the Thelma and Louise of the high seas, did their best to keep newspaper readers amused and aghast at their piratical exploits. Altitude was also achieved in 1647 by bullish land baroness Margaret Brent, who jumped over the "no suffrage for women" barrier by demanding not one but *two* votes from an astonished Maryland assembly.

From today's perspective, however, the greatest barrier broken by women during these tumultuous times was that of racism: their rebel attitudes ranged from the courage of early "underground railroad" activist Anna Douglass to the splendid insouciance of Elizabeth Mumbet Freeman, a slave who in 1783 stood up in court and demanded to be free, as spelled out in her own state's new constitution. Despite the risks, women black and white fought to bring down what was then the world's most pernicious big business — the international slave trade, which moved molasses, rum, fish, and human beings in a triangle of suffering running from Africa to the Caribbean to the American colonies.

Besides being a restless age, these centuries were times of religious flowering and revolution. North America was hip-deep in Puritans and Pilgrims, whose straitlaced rules pinched as cruelly as corsets. Thanks to Puritan persecution, witch hunts enjoyed a brief blip of popularity before disappearing. A more benign English import was Quakerism. Its exponents included remarkable go-getters like Susanna Wright and Elizabeth Haddon, who pioneered early Pennsylvania and New Jersey.

South of what North Americans would someday call "the border", a campaign of Catholicism, Spanish steel, and that Darwinian favorite, infectious disease, had flattened native cultures from the Inca to the Aztec — but not for long. Never good at taking a hint, European men had traditionally forced themselves on local women. Despite its one-sided brutality, this mating mix brought vigorous new peoples into being.

From the early 1600s on, New World women led the charge to break away from the suffocating mother countries of Spain, England, Portugal, and France. Lots of testy gals signed up to work with freedom fighters like Micaela Bastidas in Incan Peru; liberator lover Manuela Sáenz of Ecuador; and Gertrudis Bocanegra of Mexico. No matter how macho the land, daring souls like teen Rafaela Herrera of Nicaragua and Grandy Nanny, fabled rebel of British-held Jamaica, gave their all.

War continued to be a major employer. Ignoring the "No girls allowed" signs, fighting femmes found they could switch gender with a wardrobe change. Males of

4

the era wore long curls or wigs and floppy hats; their pantaloons could have hidden a cargo ship, so female hips and curves were well concealed. In Europe and both Americas, you could enlist at age fourteen, meaning there were plenty of smooth-faced, soprano-voiced soldiers in the chow lines already. Getting paid — or a pension — was another matter, however.

In the fractious colonies, the Revolutionary War attracted patriots and daredevils like Deborah Sampson and more than one "Molly Pitcher", famed for cooling cannons — and firing them. More legendary than historical was Lucy Brewer, a cross-dressing marine who allegedly saw action on the USS *Constitution* during the War of 1812. At times, being thought "a mere dame" even had its advantages: women triumphed as spies on both sides of these and other conflicts — from Lydia Darragh's gutsy peeping on the Brits to Ann Bates' peddler act, infiltrating the camps of George Washington.

In 1788, a curious sort of punitive emigration began to the land Down Under. That year, the First Fleet arrived in Australia, dumping its load of male and female "blackbirds" or convict passengers. With ten randy men to each homeless female, forced whoredom became the lot of most. Despite that barbarous beginning, determined women like Margaret Catchpole, Esther Johnston, and other now-historic jailbirds made good. A handful of highborn women *sans* fetters made equally staunch efforts to settle the land and civilize the bozos they were stuck with. Like white pioneers to other parts, most of the newcomers practiced early ethnic cleansing, nearly erasing aboriginal cultures in Australia and nearby Tasmania, even when resisted by the likes of female leaders such as Walyer and Truganini.

Not to be outdone by the men, females of this era exuberantly took up New World virtues and vices, from knocking back the new see-through champagne (its sludge removed thanks to the gallic inventiveness of winemaking widow Nicole Clicquot), to indulging in "dry inebriation" by inhaling smoke from the burning leaves of the tobacco plant. What really kept 'em breathless, however, were the stays on the corsets of the day. In the fledgling United States and elsewhere, toddlers on up were trussed like turkeys in these instruments of torture. Fashion fatalities included Elizabeth Evelyn, who died of collapsed lungs and crushed ribs — at age two.

During the first centuries of scratching a new country out of the wilderness, American women had considerable legal rights. They ran businesses, owned land, handled money, and made it. But a funny thing happened on the way to the American Revolution: women helped win in 1776 and later in 1812, but lost their own battles. Result: Female autonomy shrank faster than a corseted waistline.

By the mid-1800s, however, things looked brighter. England's Victoria, the queen of procreation, endorsed the medical use of chloroform, bringing the era of unavoidably excruciating childbirth to an end. Doctors, including Cuban Henrietta Faber, started washing their hands between patients, and mortality took a nosedive.

Women now worked away from home, in places such as garment and shoe factories; what's more, they led labor strikes to improve conditions. In 1854, a historic high-water mark was hit: 128 female postal workers in the United States now earned the same wage as their male peers.

Around that time, poet Mary Howitt (best known for her doggerel verse, "Will you walk into my parlor, said the spider to the fly") wrote the following lines:

> Let us take our proper station;
> We, the rising generation,
> Let us stamp the age as ours!

It had taken guts, and great-heartedness, and a certain grim determination. It had also taken luck — and a big dose of that female secret weapon, longevity. But uppity women around the globe had indeed carved out a brave New World for themselves.

CHAPTER
ONE

First Ladies & Superlative Travelers

SECRET CIRCUMNAVIGATOR

A Bourgogne orphan, JEANNE BARET faced major challenges from infancy. She didn't fancy starvation or child prostitution, so a disguise as a *garçon* seemed in order. Jeanne made a presentable lackey and was soon working for peanuts in Paris — but she hungered for adventure.

Mon Dieu! did she get it. Hearing about an expedition to the South Pacific, she made her way to Nantes, where two ships were being provisioned for Captain Bougainville. Their mission: a Crown-financed round-the-world trip to explore and to collect plants. Dressed to rough it, Jeanne then persuaded Philibert Commerson, the ship's botanist, that he needed a servant and go-fer. You know scientists — more interested in peering at plant sexual characteristics than human ones. Commerson hired Baret on the spot.

The good ship *L'Étoile's* first leg to Rio de Janeiro went well. In Brazil, Baret crept through jungles and waded through swamps with Commerson, searching for rare plants. They found a special one, too. Claiming it as "his own", the captain called the vine "bougainvillea". In November 1767, the ship set off again. Four scurvy-filled months later, they crawled into Tahiti. Busy watching their gums bleed, the crew still hadn't gotten hip to Jeanne's gender.

But the Tahitians knew a *wahine* when they saw one. As soon as the crew came ashore, one of the chieftains got *les hots* for Jeanne. He tried to give her a traditional welcome — the Tahitian version of the Hawaiian lei, so to speak.

After her unveiling, Jeanne had a tearful meeting with Captain Bougainville, who turned quite gallant. The French court would pardon her "crime"; meanwhile, he'd make sure she didn't have to endure anything too disagreeable. After the initial shock of learning who was washing his socks, Commerson took to Jeanne, not Jean. Years-long voyages at sea being what they are, the two were said to have become a couple. Some accounts say that they married.

Relationships aside, botanist and assistant continued to fulfill their duties. In the spring of 1769, the expedition's two ships sailed triumphantly back to France with all but nine of the original crew. Now the roster read: 200 men, 1 determined woman.

Despite having become the world's first female circumnavigator, and a pretty fair ad hoc botanist, Jeanne Baret vanished from history — though she probably stayed with Commerson until his death. Just like Jeanne, the bougainvillea plant traveled well. Its showy vines and colorful bracts now beautify warmer climes around the world.

BRAZIL'S EVE

The daughter of a Tupi Indian chief on the coast of Brazil, Bartira must have looked like a *café con leite* angel to a soggy, shipwrecked Portuguese castaway named João Ramalho. Around 1509, he washed up at what would one day be São Paulo — and had the smarts to adapt to local culture. Bartira was clever with languages. Boy, did those two communicate; in no time, they were a couple. In even less time, they were parents.

When a surprised Portuguese explorer ran into Bartira and João in 1532, they were already surrounded by many branches of their own family tree. On their own, the Ramalhos had created a harmonious mixed-race society, whose members would be called *mamelucos* by the colonizing Portuguese.

Despite being a staunch "Tupi rules" sort of girl, Bartira took a shine to Catholicism, and demanded to be baptized as BARTIRA ISABEL DIAS. She and João led an idyllic life, hosting local festivals, harvesting manioc (cassava root) as a dietary staple, and moving as free of the bizarre garments worn by later white newcomers as the first Adam and Eve.

PILGRIM PROPAGATOR

In 1620, an excited fifteen-year-old named MARY ALLERTON looked over the reeking rail of the good ship *Mayflower* at the rocky November landscape of Plymouth, Massachusetts. After the stormy misery of nine weeks spent cheek by pea-green jowl with 101 other Pilgrims, dry land looked awfully good. Granted, it was winter, and half of her companions, including her own mom, would be dead before spring, but Mary survived. Allerton was a true founding Mayflower mother: in a few years, she married, raised four kids, and helped make the Colony of New Plymouth into a thriving settlement. Mary even lived long enough to see the founding of twelve of the thirteen original colonies.

NO PAIN, NO SAINTLY GAIN

ISABEL FLORES, better known by her confirmation name of ROSE, was born in 1586. She was a half-Inca, half-Spanish kid who hung out on the streets of old Lima, Peru. Folks called her "Rose", for the flowers she raised in her parents' garden to sell around town. As a young girl, she disliked boys and thought the idea of marriage repulsive. Her role model was the saintly fourteenth-century Catherine of Siena, whose fleshly mortifications she copied. And tried to top.

Often she succeeded. During her prayer marathons, dragging a whiplash-inducing cross around her backyard, Rose dreamed up new and painful penances. The plants she worked with offered lots of ideas: nettles to line her gloves — just the thing! The shack out back gave the Peruvian teen the privacy she needed for doing her body-piercing with pieces of glass. She had the hovel nicely furnished with a pile of bricks for a bed.

One thing Rose really worried about was her looks. They were way too good. To remedy that distressing state, she ground pepper into her cheeks and dabbed on quicklime lip gloss before she jammed her homegrown crown of thorns with its sixty-nine, count 'em, sixty-nine, spikes onto her head.

But her religious vocation was more than a personal pain pilgrimage. Rose roamed the city of Lima, working to improve the lot of the poor, sick, and homeless. She

14

gave special attention to the needs of her paisanos, the suffering remnants of the Incas. Eventually she was accepted as a tertiary member (not a live-in) of the Dominican Order.

Around 1600, Rose made an important announcement to all the residents of her city: because of her prayers, she had saved Lima from a terrible earthquake. People scratched their heads and nodded: "You know, the kid's right! There hasn't been a quake — not recently, anyway." On the saintly career ladder scoreboard, up went a big "10", and Rose of Lima was on her way.

A mere half century after she expired at thirty-two, Lima's spiritual queen became the first New World-born native to be canonized. It was only a matter of years before she got tapped for another honor — becoming the patron saint for all of South America.

THE MYSTERIOUS MISS DARE

Quick: Who was the first English child born on North American soil? VIRGINIA DARE, whose mother Eleanor brought her into the New World on August 18, 1587. The place Dare popped out was an unlucky outpost called the Virginia Colony on Roanoke Island, in present-day North Carolina. When Virginia was nine days old, her grandfather John White, the leader of this hapless band, took off to England for desperately needed supplies. What with wars, sponsor bankruptcy, and so on, he didn't get back until August 1590. By then, the settlement and every one of the white colonists, baby Virginia included, had vanished. (Local Indians, some wearing smiles, were very much on the scene.) Dare, however, won a certain immortality: the island and the nearby mainland are now called Dare County in her honor.

SECOND TO NONE

In 1607, three shiploads of English colonists, all male, settled on a North American river island they named Jamestown. A year later, two rashly eager women arrived, breaking up the boys' club: MISTRESS FORREST and her maid, ANNA BURRAS, accompanied by Forrest's husband. Although the colony owed its survival to the kindly acts of Pocahontas and her Algonquin tribe, life at Jamestown was far from a cabaret. Thanks to modern archaeological detective work, we know that Mistress Forrest ate bread made from Old World wheat. It — or something, like starvation — didn't agree with her; she died in about 1609, and her 4-foot 8-inch frame was buried in a gabled coffin, very posh. Today we know what this First Lady of Jamestown looked like: a 3-D model of her head was made from a CAT scan of the skull. Expect more updates on Forrest soon. The longer-lived Anna Burras garnered firsts of her own: at fourteen, she married a working stiff named John Laydon. Their wedding was the first ever celebrated on these shores.

TAKE THESE CHAINS AND SHOVE 'EM

Arriving in Virginia in 1622 *sans* a surname, "MARY" (her slave handle) drew an owner who raised tobacco. Despite the dawn-to-dusk routine on the plantation, Mary soon found a man to love in fellow slave Anthony.

At that time, Virginia was home to only a few hundred African souls. With brutally hard work, incredible luck, and/or the goodwill of a white landowner, slaves could become freedmen and -women. Theoretically. As court records in Northampton County show, Mary and Tony pulled it off. They became the first free blacks in the United States, with the right to choose their own surname.

Now known as the Johnsons, they found their own chunk of heaven. By mid-century, these workaholics possessed 250 acres, cattle, pigs, and four kids. In 1653, a fire nearly wiped them out — but more luck: white neighbors helped them. Then MARY JOHNSON petitioned local officials, who had an inexplicably mellow moment and granted her tax-exempt status for life!

In their steady climb towards early yuppiedom, the Johnsons moved to Maryland, leased 300 acres, and named it Tonies Vineyard. The kids, now grown, took up farming nearby. Their presence made things easier for Mary when her husband keeled over. She herself kept on ticking until her late sixties.

Her descendants wouldn't be so fortunate. As the demand for cheap labor grew in the colonies, it was answered by a huge jump in the importation of black slaves — called New Africans — rather than indentured white servants from Europe. The upward mobility and basic civil rights of free blacks ebbed to the vanishing point.

MORE PRINCELY FIRSTS

Back then, few journalists would have considered it a "scoop", but MARY PRINCE, born in the West Indies around 1788, had a compelling first: her autobiographical book that detailed human slavery and suffering in the Caribbean. Its title: *The History of Mary Prince, a West Indian Slave*. Its pub date? 1831. She came to write it after living in London, writing for the *Anti-Slavery Reporter*, beginning around 1827. Despite these accomplishments, frustratingly little is known about her.

She wasn't the only boatrocker named MARY PRINCE. An earlier and paler nonconformist by that name arrived at Boston in 1656, along with seven other Quakers. She immediately made herself Prince non grata by denouncing the Puritan ministers who were part of the greeting-cum-interrogation party. Among other things, this plainspoken firebrand called them "hirelings and seed of the serpent".

TOUR-JETTÉING TO THE TOP

From her very first *battement tendu*, Paris-born SUZANNE VAILLANDE DOUVILLIER loved to dance. She became a ballet star in France, but wanted to be a celeb in toe shoes on another continent. Touring. That was it. "Book me one of those international tours," she demanded. "Just make sure they've got Perrier in the dressing rooms!" Suzanne captivated audiences in New York, Philadelphia, and New Orleans. Pretty soon her agent reported, "You're a star in the United States!"

Never content with the status quo, Suzanne told herself, "*Moi*, I must outrage." Thus, in 1808, she took the lead role in an American ballet. The ballet itself wasn't scandalous; her role, however — as the male lead — was. Now that she had the distinctions of first ballet cross-dresser and first ballerina star in the United States under her tutu, Vaillande frantically sought other superlatives to make life worth living. As her joints aged, Suzanne began to dance less and direct other dancers more, inadvertently becoming America's first female choreographer.

THE COURTROOM — IT'S MY LIFE

An English Catholic family rolling in assets and arrogance, the Brents arrived at Maryland colony in 1638: two brothers and two sisters, MARGARET and MARY BRENT. "Now what?" they asked each other. "Time to start our own feudal system, of course!" Founded by Catholic Lord Baltimore, Maryland only had a few hundred whites huddled on its shores, so enticements to colonize were juicy: a thousand-acre manor for anyone who paid ship's passage and maintenance for able-bodied males to work the land.

Once Margaret and Mary met Lord Baltimore, they established Sisters Freehold, raising livestock and adding another thousand acres here and there to their holdings by bringing over as many nicely buffed male workers as they could.

Things got much more exciting in 1647, when Lord Baltimore's bigwig brother Lord Calvert died, having named Margaret executrix of his estate. For encores, she was also given power of attorney for the absent Lord Baltimore. Yahoo! The following year she coolly marched into the Maryland Assembly and said, "Besides calling me 'Lord' Maggie from now on, I've decided you've got to let me do as you chaps do and vote. Of course, I'll need to get *two* votes on everything — one as your major landholder, and the other as an executrix."

What a faux pas. Brent's ignorance of the simple fact that females could not vote left the members aghast. The Assembly said no, of course; whereupon Margaret did a pretty good imitation of Al Pacino in a courtroom, ranting, "Out of order! This assembly is out of order! This *colony* is out of order!"

Although she was never able to finesse the double-vote thing — drat! — Maggie loved law and did spend a lot of time in court, both as plaintiff and as *in pro per* attorney for her friends — who were only too willing to let Brent do the blowhard dealing.

Ultimately the sibling tag team of Brents left Maryland in 1651 — the darn place was getting just rotten with Puritans anyway — and settled in Virginia, where Margaret ruled the roost at a plantation called Peace until she was a robust seventy-one.

IN PHOTOGRAPHY WE TRUST

None of this hide-it-under-the-mattress stuff for CLARA KEATON: when a newfangled outfit calling itself a "bank" opened in Baltimore in the 1830s, this canny queen of thrift headed up the queue. In doing so, she became the National Savings and Trust Bank's first depositor. Daring Clara was a handsome black woman. Her photograph, showing her dressed for the occasion in her best bonnet and shawl, still reposes at Howard University. Clara's image still looks good. Odds are, it's probably held up better than the institution she entrusted with her legal tender.

WHY MAY 26 SHOULD BE MARY MONTAGU DAY

Quicksilver LADY MARY WORTLEY MONTAGU lived B.E.J. — before Edward Jennings. Credited as the "smallpox savior", vaccinator Jennings was merely putting his Wellingtons in the far-ranging footsteps of this outrageous intellectual. While living in Turkey with her ambassador husband, Mary learned about the local custom of inoculating healthy folks against smallpox, using a mild form of the live virus.

In 1719, she brought the method back to England, immunizing her own daughter first. Later, she convinced the royal family to vaccinate others, including their own daughters.

Predictably, doctors of the day hated inoculation — not that *they* had any solution for 60 million smallpox deaths annually. But Lady Mary — herself a deeply scarred survivor of the disease — persisted. Witty, literate, and great at networking (her 900-letter correspondence was later published), she was as effective as any epidemic in popularizing the measure. By the 1750s, immunization had crossed the ocean and was saving lives in the American colonies as well.

Although Mary became nearly as well known for her saucy tongue and her international amours, her contribution to world health remains immense. By the time Lady Montagu died in 1762, the death rate from smallpox had dropped from 30 percent to 2 percent — a legacy well worth honoring annually, don't you think?

MASS MOVEMENT

In the late 1700s, a female slave known simply as BELINDA noticed that the newly established state of Massachusetts had formed a legislature. And it was to this legislature that she petitioned for freedom from slavery. Her petition still exists, and makes its case eloquently: "I have not yet enjoyed the benefits of creation," Belinda said, "and I beg for freedom." Did first petitioner Belinda get her demands met? This we don't know for certain.

However, her actions did inspire another slave, ELIZABETH MUMBET FREEMAN, to act. In her forties when the Massachusetts constitution came into being, Elizabeth caught wind of the state bill of rights about "all men being born free and equal". Hmm. Could "women" be substituted for "men"? It was worth a shot. She ran away from her abusive master, found a Ralph Nader-esque lawyer who sympathized, and took it to the state jurisdiction. After Theodore Sedgwick pleaded her case, Elizabeth found she'd won 30 shillings in damages from her former owner. And, oh yes, her freedom. She'd also waltzed into a job as a servant to her lawyer ("But . . . I thought you were working my case *pro bono!*").

At least Mumbet was paid enough as a servant to eventually buy her own house. In that home, with her daughter, Mrs. Freeman lived as a free woman and a citizen of Massachusetts until the grand old age of eighty-seven.

TALE OF TWO LITERATES

Publisher of almanacs and newspapers in two states. First postmaster of Baltimore. Printer of the first signed copy of the Declaration of Independence. Sounds like Ben Franklin, but it was a lifelong single woman named MARY KATHERINE GODDARD. What's more, Mary's formidable mother, SARAH UPDIKE GODDARD, printed and published, too.

Mom and daughter came from old families that had settled in Rhode Island and Long Island. Despite the handicap of an unusually good education, including studies in Latin and French, Sarah Updike married a doctor when she hit thirty-five.

You know doctors — they never take care of themselves. Sarah eventually found herself widowed but well-cushioned with a decent legacy. She immediately loaned half of it to son William to start a printing press and newspaper in Providence. Billy, however, could never win enough subscribers, and, darn it, that Stamp Tax took the fun out of business. He abandoned ship and machinery in 1765, whereupon Mom, in her fifties, and sister Mary Katherine sprang into action. While Mary got her first taste of slapping ink on paper, Sarah turned the *Providence Gazette* into a moneymaker, eventually selling it on the upswing. Bibliophile Sarah also ran a bookshop, added luster to her reputation by doing custom bookbinding, and took on select publishing projects. She brought out the first American edition of *The Letters of Lady Mary Montagu*, the literate humanitarian who'd brought smallpox vaccination to Europe and the American colonies.

Wouldn't you know it, Billy popped up again, needing another fiscal transfusion; this time, he wanted to start the *Pennsylvania Chronicle*. Sarah put in capital (and untold hours, managing the business) until she was seventy. Finally, this grand old lady of print managed to get off the hook — but she had to die to do it.

Meanwhile, Mary Katherine had become a talented printer, editor, and type compositor. Like mom, she took over one of Billy's startups — the *Baltimore Journal* — when he abandoned it for "other offers". Even during the paper-scarce days of the Revolutionary War, she got the *Journal* out — and scooped her competitors.

In 1777, she won the honor of publishing the "true copies" of the Declaration of Independence, the first time the document was signed by the signatories. (As a freebie, Mary Katherine paid couriers to deliver the Declaration throughout the thirteen colonies!) Between print jobs, Goddard squeezed in an almanac or two, ran her own bookstore, and became Baltimore's first postmaster.

At times Mary paid postal workers out of her own pocket, in coin. That hurt — especially when others in business, including the fledgling government, paid in more easily devalued paper currency or even in barter goods, such as tobacco or fish. After fourteen years running the post office, Mary K. lost her job. Cutbacks? Hardly. Now that it was a cushy federal post with a travel expense account, bureaucrats thought the job "too difficult for a woman".

Instead of wallowing in murderous fantasies, Goddard retired to her bookstore, where she lived to be a sane and hearty seventy-eight.

SHE ♥ NEW YORK

KATY FERGUSON was born a slave in transit, on a schooner carrying her enslaved mother from Virginia to New York. Separated from her mom by the cruelties of slavery at age eight, the child became a member of the Murray Street Church. In her teens, she got a windfall: a generous woman laid out $200 to free Katy. Despite losing her husband and babies to illness, despite low-paying work as a caterer and laundress, Ferguson spent the next sixty years doing good works around the Big Apple. Among her sterling accomplishments: setting up the first Sunday School in the city; caring for forty-eight foster children; and working with unwed mothers, black and white, to find good homes for themselves and their offspring. It took cholera to carry off this stalwart eighty-year-old in 1854. In 1920, the city of New York finally recognized Katy Ferguson, and in appreciation, opened a home for unwed mothers named after this selfless woman.

THE ARTIST FIRST KNOWN AS PRINCE

Heads-up for Trivial Pursuit fans: It was LUCY TERRY PRINCE, not Phillis Wheatley, who clocked in as America's first black poet.

Lucy began life in Africa, was sold as a slave to Ebenezer Wells, and ended up in Deerfield, Massachusetts. An Indian attack in 1746 on two neighboring families inspired her to write. Although her rhyming poem called "The Bars Fight" might sound like a tavern brawl, "The Bars" was a meadow where the battle took place.

Poetry was merely one facet of Lucy's eventful life. She married a free black man named Abijah Prince, whose thoughtful wedding gift was probably her own emancipation. After moving to Guilford, Vermont, the Princes raised six children.

Lucy continued her bootstrap education. Generous but no pushover, Prince used her abilities to pursue legal claims and rights for herself, her family, and friends. When hostile white neighbors threatened the family, Lucy and Abijah took it to the Vermont Governor and Council. When one of her sons wanted to enroll in Williams College, Lucy orated for three hours, using biblical scripture, legal precedent, and other means to plead his case before the trustees. She lost the case — but earned their deep admiration.

Around 1800, trouble arose again; this time, a crooked colonel tried to steal land from the Princes. Although she was now pushing seventy, Lucy went all the way to the Supreme Court. Against two prominent attorneys, she pled her case before Judge Samuel Chase — who said that Prince made a better argument than any he'd ever heard from Vermont members of the bar! The stout-hearted matriarch won, and retired to the family farm. It must have agreed with her: she lived into her nineties.

COULDN'T GET A FOOTE IN THE DOOR

She was only twelve, but precocious LUCINDA FOOTE could already boast a number of notable entries on her curriculum vitae. Even more gratifying, she'd already been turned down by the finest institution of higher learning in the land — Yale University. The current prez of Yale, Ezra Stiles, had interviewed the brilliant preteen himself. Instead of giving her a chance to matriculate, he gave her an early Christmas present on December 22, 1783: a glowing — albeit misspelled — testimonial.

The girl was no doubt thrilled to read, "Let it be known unto you, that I have tested Miss Lucinda Foote, aged 12, by way of examination, proving that she has made laudable progress in the languages of the learned, viz, the Latin and the Greek; to such an extent that I found her translating and expounding with perfick (sic) ease, both words and sentences in the whole of Virgil's *Aeneid*, in selected orations of Cicero, and in the Greek (New) testament. I testify that were it not for her sex, she would be considered fit to be admitted as a student in the freshman class of Yale University."

Still, Stiles felt a tiny twinge of . . . something. When he wasn't busy developing debate topics for Yale seniors such as "Whether Women Ought to Be Permitted to Partake in Civil Government Dominion", he tutored Lucinda — following the Yale curriculum, of course.

Yale's first female reject went on to a career as dutiful wife, mother of ten, and private person — but what a waste to the world.

But She's Just Not
Hahvahd Material!

Clever, intensely interested in medicine, and from a supportive Boston family, HARRIOT KEZIA HUNT began her medical studies with an herbalist in about 1824. Eleven years later, after working with established doctors as well, she hung out her shingle in Boston as a physician. As she wryly noted, "If I'd had cholera or smallpox, I could not have been more avoided than I was."

Harriot longed for more profound medical instruction than she'd been able to obtain. Frankly, she was dying to cut open a cadaver or two. Above all, she wanted to learn more about physiology, so she could prevent disease, not merely treat it. As she wrote, "That word — *preventive* — seemed a great word to me; curative was small beside it . . ."

Impressed with her professionalism, her own patients urged her to apply to the medical lecture program at Harvard University, a male bastion since its inception in 1636. Hunt's first application was flatly rejected. A few years later, she tried again. No soap. Finally, in 1850, with the support of people like Oliver Wendell Holmes, and with the words of the first national women's rights convention ringing in her ears, Harriot applied again.

The school smoothly said, "We *could* allow you to attend medical lectures — but of course you cannot

37

earn a degree." A heartbeat later, the entire student body met in a fury, passing a resolution against the whole notion of Hunt's presence. Among the gems they put into print: "We are not opposed to allowing woman her rights, but do protest against her appearing in places where her presence is calculated to destroy our respect for the modesty and delicacy of her sex."

By now in her forties, and in a pretty good-sized dudgeon, Harriot Hunt shot off to the Women's Medical College in Philadelphia for the advanced training she craved. Later she wrote about her putative colleagues, saying, "The 1851 class of Harvard has purchased for themselves a notoriety they will not covet in years to come."

YANKEE HOT AIR

In the balloon-happy United States, aerostation-worshipping women were as suicidally daring as their European counterparts. Inspired by the kamikaze feats of France's Marie Blanchard, on October 24, 1825, MADAME JOHNSON made a solo flight from Castle Garden, a pleasure park in New York City. The "fair voyager", as she was dubbed by newspaper reporters, landed in a Long Island salt marsh. After her maiden voyage, Johnson enjoyed three years of successful gas balloon launches in New Jersey, New York, and Pennsylvania. The biggest hang-up with ballooning in Johnson's day was the high cost of inflating the envelope with hydrogen gas. Would-be flyers had to have fat checkbooks — or do pay-per-view. Johnson had a firm policy. If she didn't take in enough at the gate, she wouldn't go up. Her resolve set off several near-riots in Philadelphia and Manhattan.

Always a hotbed of hot air — and ballooning, too — Philadelphia boasted its own female aeronaut, called MADAME DELON. On the morning of June 25, 1856, two seasoned aeronauts helped her inflate her balloon. Then Delon lifted off from the corner of Callowhill and Seventh Streets, headed over the Delaware River, and sailed sedately over four villages before landing safely at Tacony in time for dinner. Her time aloft — more than seven hours — caused amazement. (Almost as amazing was the fact that avid reporters neglected to note the first names of either Delon or Johnson!)

NETWORKING — IT'S MY LIFE

Verbal verve — that's what New Hampshire-born SARAH BAGLEY had in abundance. She put it to good use, too, as the first union organizer for women in the United States. In addition to a talent for fiery oratory, Sarah had a profound belief in the rights of working women, and a writer's way with words. It takes real eloquence to motivate people when you're saying things like: "We need to fight for a ten-hour workday!" (Back then, workdays ran twelve hours or more, six days a week.)

She first became an activist in 1836, in Lowell, Massachusetts. Sarah was everywhere: buttonholing politicians to hold public hearings on working conditions; teaching free classes to other woman mill workers; organizing a union with regional reach; seeing that her union took over a publication called the *Voice of Industry* to give more accurate reportage on factory life. Heck, she barely had time to put in her twelve hours a day at the textile mill. Bagley devoted ten years to union organizing. In recognition, she was blacklisted for her activities. Ever the communicator, she resurfaced elsewhere as a telegraph operator — again, the first woman ever to win that job.

CHAPTER
TWO

Spies & She-Merchants

LIGHT SPYING AND GRAVER MATTERS

A tiny Irishwoman, intelligent, flexible, and full of fight, LYDIA DARRAGH landed in Philadelphia with her growing family in the mid-1700s. Lydia loved to doctor people. A midwife of note, she had lots of hands-on practice and herbal common sense as well.

However, she may have done more business at the other end of the life/death continuum, judging by her 1766 ad in the *Pennsylvania Gazette:* "Lydia Darragh, living in Second Street, at the corner of Taylor's Alley, opposite the Golden Fleece Tavern, takes this method of informing the Public that she intends to make Grave-Clothes, and lay out the Dead, in the Neatest Manner . . . she hopes, by her Care, to give Satisfaction to those who will be pleased to favour her with their Orders."

A Quaker like her husband William, Lydia quietly carried off major heroics during the Revolutionary War.

When the British occupied the city, they commandeered a room in the Darragh house to hold strategy meetings. Lydia and company weren't asked to vacate — just go up to bed, and stay there, were the orders. (The Brits assumed that, being Quaker pacifists, the Darraghs would be neutral. Ha!)

At first, spying was a family affair: when Lydia got a juicy bit of news, her husband wrote it in shorthand. Then she hid it inside one or more big buttons, sewed them on her younger son's jacket, and had him deliver the data to her older son, who was serving in the Army at Washington's camp.

On the night of December 2, 1777, the British held a super-secret skull session. Lydia listened at the door — and heard a bombshell: British troops were going to attack the Americans at Whitemarsh in three days! Mild-mannered Lydia devised a daring plan. First she wangled a pass to go through British lines, saying that the family needed flour. After walking five miles to the mill, she found a Yankee scout, passed on her information (hidden in a piece of needlework), grabbed her flour, and booked it for home.

Shortly thereafter, the Redcoats took a royal whipping at that battle — and a suspicious officer came to interrogate Lydia. Luckily, like many a prosecuting attorney, he asked her the wrong questions, so she didn't have to lie. This greathearted patriot in a small package lived until 1789. (But not as a Quaker — the local Society of Friends expelled the Darraghs and their older son for being altogether too martial.) When she died, the town responded with a fulsome obituary, a well-attended funeral, and — one hopes — someone to lay her out "in the nearest manner", as Lydia Darragh herself would have done.

PELT AND PRUNE MAVEN

Even as a young sprout in the Netherlands, MARGARET HARDENBROECK knew her math — and human nature. This paragon of independence and business acumen sailed *sans* clan across the Atlantic in 1659. She settled in New Amsterdam, the first of her entrepreneurial family to venture to the Dutch colony.

Once on dry land, Margaret quickly set herself up in the import/export business, trading furs from the New World for cooking oil, vinegar, and pins from the Old. On one of her slow trading days, she married a merchant named Pieter Rudolphus DeVries, a fellow who'd already made a respectable number of guilders in the city. Motherhood made its appearance, but Margaret continued to work the fur trade, while Pieter shipped tobacco, sugar, bricks, wine, and prunes. (As if plague and smallpox weren't enough — irregularity had also reared its ugly head in early New York.)

In less than two years, her husband gave up the ghost, leaving Margaret morose but not bereft. She and baby daughter Maria inherited his real estate and business, down to the last prune. The widow kept busy, suing and being sued, until 1663, when she wed a second Dutch trader, Frederick Philipse. As in her previous marriage, under Dutch law she kept her legal rights and other prerogatives, including the use of her maiden name for business.

In their twenty-odd years together, canny Margaret and slick Fred put together their own shipping fleet, including his and her *Marge* and *Freddie* vessels. Since Margaret traveled for free on their ships, she shuttled often between America and Holland.

In 1664, she got off the boat to some bad news. The blasted British had beat the clogs off the Dutch, and now were in charge of the 9,000 inhabitants of New Amsterdam, which they had renamed New York. Big deal. The Brits needed prunes even more than the Dutch, Margaret thought.

What really hurt were those antiquated English laws. From now on, she couldn't buy real estate in her own name; she couldn't even do a decent power of attorney. The couple continued to pile up humongous amounts of profits, property, ships, and other toys, but Margaret remained in a real huff about the whole thing until her death in 1691.

Hardenbroeck didn't know how lucky she was to live when she did. Within forty years of her death, the law got draconian: a New York widow had to forfeit *all* of her first husband's property if she ever married again!

I WANNA BE IN ESCROW!

Shocking as it may sound, many a woman hungered for her very own real estate in the New World — *and* got it. Among the land baronesses: ELIZABETH POOLE, who founded the town of Taunton, Massachusetts, out of her holdings.

In the early 1700s, Maine was one big hunk of terrain, no subdivisions, no nothing. A handful of colonists owned the whole thing — among them John Hancock, Samuel Adams, and a very smart cookie named ABIGAIL BROMFIELD.

Certain Eastern seaboard places were already "in" — and others, already "out". Take a small Massachusetts island variously called Chopoquidic or Chappaquiddick. Even though it was within spitting distance of popular Martha's Vineyard, its owner, MARCY CHESSE, decided to dump her island in 1771. The stress of spelling it over and over? A premonition on Marcy's part? You decide.

ISN'T IT ALWAYS ABOUT LOCATION?

Rhode Islander ABIGAIL STONEMAN was bursting with bright ideas for businesses. Between 1768 and 1774, just before a larger enterprise called the "United States of America" got off the ground, Abigail opened her doors to the public six times. Her game plan: to cater to the new vices of the colonial populace. The Merchant's Coffee House, her first caffeine emporium, won a quick following. Ditto her genteel teahouse. Building on beverage success, Abigail next became a tavern keeper. Then, seeing the driving-impaired state her clientele reached by the wee hours, Mrs. Stoneman provided another service: a boarding-house. But venturesome Abby may have gone a startup or two too far. Aiming to fulfill the dancing needs of her community, she opened a ballroom in Newport, then extended her coffeehouse franchise to latte-swilling Boston. The locale she chose, however, was enough to twang already-jangled nerves. Abigail's new java hut sat smack on the still-bloodstained site of the Boston Massacre.

NOT CHEAP, BUT I'M WORTH IT

DIONIS COFFIN hankered to make her own beer. Not just any old swill — topnotch brew for the discerning colonist. Who knew she would have a legal fight on her hands? Considering the amount of publicity it got her, perhaps she set about this deliberately.

It all began when desirable Dionis of Devon, England, married Tristam Coffin. Three kids later, the Quaker couple emigrated to the thirsty, amenity-free colony of Massachusetts in 1642.

After settling in Newbury, Dionis and Tristam opened a tavern in the town. By 1652 or so, Mrs. Coffin was brewing her popular spruce beer. Even at 3 pence a quart, it went fast. But what's this? Those wet blankets, the city fathers, issued Dionis a summons in 1653, charging her with overcharging. Well, Mistress Coffin was one brewer who wasn't about to back down.

Dionis had her day in court, producing various witnesses who swore that she put six bushels of malt into each hogshead of brew — a full two more than the standard recipe called for. Thus, she proclaimed, her spruce beer was worth more. After deliberation, and perhaps two or three sample mugs, the court agreed, and Dionis walked.

But the bloom was off Newbury, as far as the Coffins were concerned. They toyed with living in Salisbury, then settled on Nantucket Island in 1660, where Dionis and Tristam set about bringing their children-count up to nine. Their descendants, thanks in no small part to finer beer, multiplied and spread like crabgrass. Today you'll find Coffins in every state and English-speaking country around the globe. What you won't find is much in the way of good spruce beer.

AGENT 355, WHERE ARE YOU?

During the Revolutionary War years of 1775-1781, patriotic women did their ingenious best to thwart the Brits. In places such as New York, where the Redcoats occupied U.S. territory for long periods, women played a key role in spying.

Because Long Island linked New York and Connecticut, it became the epicenter for complex spying operations. One of the most organized had ANNA STRONG as a strategic member.

By happy chance, this matron's property at Strong's Neck was close to water channels. Her job: to read lantern signal lights each night. And to signal back by day, using the innocent-appearing device of garments hanging from the washline. Strong communicated where messages awaited, and in which inlet they were hidden. A black petticoat plus a number of white handkerchiefs on Anna's line might mean "There's a message in inlet five". (It could also mean that flu season had hit.)

Going about their everyday activities, taking eats and supplies to relatives, and hanging out laundry to dry, Anna and other operatives carried out assignments. For once, being underestimated was a blessing. Females could run documents in and out of New York City much more easily than men could.

Homey as these spy doings might seem to a Ludlum-jaded reader, it was dangerous work. One of Anna's cohorts, known only as SPY 355, was captured by the Redcoats in 1779. For her, and other prisoners on the British vessel *Jersey*, imprisonment was a one-way trip — a sacrifice still largely unacknowledged.

SPY WANTED: MATH SKILLS A MUST

ANN BATES was raising a few bees and teaching the ABCs in Philadelphia when conflict arose. Enraged parents? PTA turf issues? No — a war for independence. Ann was incensed; ungrateful colonists! Why couldn't they just knuckle under to British royalty, as any sane person had done for centuries? In 1778, Loyalist Bates made a move. Kissing her gun-repair military mate good-bye, she scuttled her schoolmarming for a spot of spying.

As peddler Ann, she infiltrated Yankee military camps, selling combs, knives, and medicinal rhubarb to the women with the army. Bates moved freely from one camp to the next. While making change and small talk, Ann counted cannons, food supplies, and manpower, and gloated over her thespian talents. Using secret signs and tokens (how delicious!), she passed her data to other Loyalists working undercover in Washington's army.

Over time, however, espionage proved rather high-stress. Fearless Ann didn't mind fording rivers, staying in scruffy "safe houses" — or even the occasional strip search. Several times she even bluffed American commanders into letting her go free. Trouble was, she got no rest between spy missions. In a couple of years, the Yanks were on to her — and her nerves were shredded. Prudently retiring her cloak and dagger,

Ann went to rejoin her armorer hubby in the newly British bastion of Charleston, South Carolina.

When the whole sorry debacle was over, the Bateses retreated to England, along with many other Loyalists. There, needy and indignant, Ann spent the rest of her years fighting the British — trying to collect on the fine fees she'd been promised for her 007-ing. Her eloquent dunning letters still exist. In one, she says, "Haid I Doon half as much for the Scruff of Mankind, I mean the Rabls, I Should not be thus Left to Parish." An irony indeed — doncha *love* this quote! — no matter what you think of her spelling, for the woman who'd been called "the most successful spy in history".

AN EIGHTEENTH-CENTURY "THIRD PLACE"

The phrase "Colonial inn" might summon up thoughts of an early B&B to us; but to travelers and locals in the 1700s, the innkeeper and her establishment offered an amazing array of services. The Charlestown inn of JANE ELDRIDGE, for instance. Besides the food, drink, and lodging she provided, her place was a coffeehouse and the site of musical events, balls, assemblies, and fancy suppers. Want to see a cockfight? Make a quick pick on a local lottery? Rendezvous for a midnight duel or a midday quickie? Eldridge's inn was your answer. Innkeepers like Jane acted as local lost-and-founds, rented out vehicles from coaches to saddle horses, and allowed others to buy and sell on the premises. In fact, there wasn't much you couldn't do at her place. The tax collectors met regularly at Eldridge's. Jane even hosted the funeral of the local governor!

CURB APPEAL

She may have been young and saddled with two kids, but widow-in-training MARY SPRATT ALEXANDER knew a thing or two about customers. Her dowry had gone into late mate Sam's import firm; she'd helped run it until he bit the dust.

Since there was little chance of putting up a Web site, she pondered how to expand her business. Then it came to her: increase foot traffic. Her offices were on one street, her countinghouse on another — so Mary outlined her properties with large flat stones.

New Yorkers came to buy — and to ogle the Big Apple's first sidewalk. Pretty soon Mary's high-and-dry was a tourist attraction. Even after she remarried, Mary prospered, contracting to supply armies with the early American version of Spam and other foodstuffs. Later, she and second husband Jim bought a spread in Perth Amboy, upstate. There, empathetic Mary made friends with her Native American neighbors; by the end of her life in 1760, she was known — among the Indians, no less! — as a medicine woman.

TRANSATLANTIC HEAD TRIP

PATIENCE LOVELL WRIGHT was poorly named. *Im*patience might have been more apropos (some who knew her well might vote for "talented wacko"). Born in Bordentown, New Jersey, in 1725, she dabbled in wax for years. Not candles — wax heads. Patience could sculpt a divine Greek goddess — not that she had much time, between the Quaker church, her husband, and five kids.

Then two tragedies made mincemeat of her life. Her spouse died poor. Worse yet, she turned forty-seven. With a family to support, Mrs. Wright decided: enough of these wan wax Athenas. She'd do celebrity heads. Her sister helped her move to New York, work up a traveling exhibit, and take her show to London, where they really appreciated that stuff. By 1772, after her buddy Ben Franklin introduced her into society, Patience was on the fast track.

Patience was no artistic flash in the pan. She waxed the greats and near-greats of her day, on both sides of the Atlantic. (Her most famous work, a spookily life-sized number of Prime Minister William Pitt, still startles visitors to Westminster Abbey.)

Nob after nob commissioned work; England's king and queen even took to dropping by her studio. Dressed in raggedy garb as casual as her speech, Patience called the royals "George" and "Charlotte" — when she wasn't swearing a blue streak.

Few knew that Wright was keen to try her hand as a spy. From an unsigned letter praising her patriotic activities, it seems likely that Mrs. W chatted up her subjects as she modeled their waxen heads on her lap. Disarmed by her patter, unsuspecting clients let down their hair — and Patience learned much of strategic value for the Americans. With the Revolutionary War looming, they needed it. And what could be simpler than for the sculptor to stick a note inside the craniums of the commissions she shipped to the United States? Since she owed Ben Franklin a big one, it was probably to him that she reported on British moves while loudly maintaining her pro-British, anti-war stance.

At length, Mrs. Wright wearied of London and hit Paris with her creative services. There she ran into *another* wax whiz named Marie Tussaud, whose name would soar worldwide to become synonymous with celebrity likenesses. Wrong timing for a Wright idea.

CASHABLE ART

From an innkeeper's family, MARY PECK BUTTERWORTH lived at the Sign of the Black Horse in Rehoboth, a pokey village between the Massachusetts and Rhode Island colonies. Saddled with a contractor mate and a spate of seven young 'uns, she was doomed, it seemed, to the ho-hum of housewifedom.

But La Butterworth was an artiste. Secretly, she began experimenting with inks, quill pens, and materials. One night, it all came together: she created her own money. To be more precise, Mary made copies of the paper currencies from three colonies that were small masterpieces.

Then her *true* genius surfaced. She invented the first disposable plate for counterfeiting, fashioned from the stiff muslin of her own petticoats! Brilliantly simple: She wet a piece of muslin, ironed it over a bill, and the image appeared on the cloth. After transferring the image to a piece of paper, she cut it to size — and threw the incriminating muslin into the fire. This was no mass-production Warhol operation, however; to make the bogus bills passable, Mary spent hours tracing each line with a quill pen.

Her business acumen matched her artistry. To distribute her growing cache of funny money, the kitchen entrepreneur enlisted her three brothers, several neighbors, a deputy sheriff, *and* a signup list from her own church, the Congregational Meetinghouse. Before long, Mary had to train another forger, and found a neat-handed apprentice in her sister-in-law, HANNAH PECK.

Mrs. B's counterfeiting ring ran silky-smooth for seven years, her bucks passing as legal tender in places high and low around New England. But then a careless confederate passed a Butterworth when he shouldn't have — and a keen-eyed innkeeper called the cops.

One August day in 1723, sheriffs with warrants hauled Mary Butterworth and some of her accomplices away to a jail in Bristol, Rhode Island. Their exclamations of "We broke the case!" were premature, however. The police couldn't get — and never got — any physical evidence of the ringleader's criminal activities.

Butterworth and her brother Israel went free. Frustrated, the local gendarmes kept her under surveillance for years — but the demure inventor (to their knowledge) never picked up pen or muslin again.

WHEN YOU HAVE LEMONS . . .

Born in a low-rent part of Mexico in 1768, EULALIA PÉREZ wanted outta there, and married the first uniform that came along.

The new Señora de Guillén and Miguel pointed the burro north to the then smog-free skies of southern California. Three kids and twenty-some years later, they ended up at Mission San Juan Capistrano. Eulalia was heavily pregnant. Again. On December 8, 1812, she was enjoying Mass at the mission church when *la madre* of all quakes hit. Eulalia was buried under the rubble of walls and roof. Fortunately, she wasn't one of the forty who were mashed into guacamole by the huge mission bells. She crawled out, and a couple of days later had a healthy baby girl.

What with quakes and pregnancies, Eulalia wasn't that enchanted with Capistrano or Miguel. But it took nine years of nagging her soldier to get him to move to San Gabriel, where he promptly died.

Confronted with her large and hungry brood, the marital survivor entered a cooking contest — and won. The prize? A job as cook for the palate-conscious friars of Mission San Gabriel. With her experience in personnel management (those kids!), Eulalia soon was running the place, supervising the making of wine and olive oil, and trying vainly to keep soldiers away from the Indian women. Her biggest challenge: figuring out

61

what to do with all the citrus the mission orchards produced.

Just for fun, Eulalia took up lemonade manufacture. Before long, she had to bottle the stuff, the demand was so great. The friars saw they had a hit on their hands — Pérez coolers became one of Los Angeles's first exports. Despite the shipping costs, thirsty Spain was a big customer.

Although Señora became known as *la reina de limonada*, the queenly profits from the sale of the citrus drink went to the mission, not to her. After fourteen years on the job, Eulalia got a pink slip from the brand-new Mexican government of California: "So sorry, missions being secularized; kiss your *limonada adiós*."

The padres felt bad, and gave Eulalia a golden handshake: 14,500 acres of land in what would be Pasadena today. At the eleventh hour, the friars stressed over technicalities: omigod, we didn't notice, Eulalia's female. Did women count when it came to land grants? Then a padre with salsa for brains suggested: "Let's find the old gal a new husband, and grant the land to *him!* Yeah!" In a frenzy, they rounded up Juan Marine, a young soldier.

Although a bit titillated by her older-woman-with-younger-stud status, Eulalia soon walked out on Juan, disgusted by his bossiness and sloth. Eschewing both wedlock and property, she took up residence in a tiny adobe near the old mission. It was a place she enjoyed for the rest of her mostly vigorous years, entertained by her huge clan, her kidneys washed by an ample supply of the best lemonade California had to offer: her own.

"DEAL THE NEXT HAND, RED!"

You always had to keep your eyes on the hands of TULES GERTRUDES BARCELÓ when you were sitting at her gambling table in old Santa Fe, in the province of New Mexico. Usually called "La Tules", this *simpática* redhead came from a family background of wealth. But she'd run away from the hick town of Tome, and an unhappy marriage, to make it on her own — a highly unusual scenario for a Mexican woman, then or now.

In the 1830s, La Tules opened what was probably Santa Fe's most popular establishment, a classy gambling saloon and dance hall on the main plaza of the city. It became the nerve center of politics and community life. Barceló presided over the place, often dealing cards at the monte bank table — one of the ways in which she became rich on her own. No help needed from husband or family!

By the 1840s, when Mexico and the United States went to war, La Tules had become an ex officio political adviser. Both sides sought the opinions of the sage at the center of local society. Barceló lived to see New Mexico become a U.S. territory, and her story, embellished and romanticized at times, has been told in poetry, song, and novels like *The Wind Leaves No Shadow*.

NICOTINE FRINGES

Enterprising women found jobs aplenty in the colonies of Virginia, Georgia, Maryland, and North Carolina. Some were far from traditionally feminine. At times, the pay stank — but not precisely in the way you'd think.

With the scarcity of bridges in the New World, the ferryboat business boomed. Female innkeepers and planters often took on the additional job of maintaining ferry service across nearby rivers. For instance, in Bristol Parish, Virginia, ELIZABETH KENNON was ferry mistress for fifteen years, beginning in 1720. Her annual salary amounted to 2,500 pounds — that's tobacco, not £ sterling.

A Maryland woman by the name of ELIZABETH SKINNER won a similar gig. The requirements for the job, which was administered by the court in Talbot County, stated "that she would keep a good boat fit for such use and transport the inhabitants of the County, their horses and carriages, over Oxford ferry ... as often as they shall have occasion". The county set the ferry tolls that Skinner would receive, and in addition paid her 4,900 pounds of the noxious weed a year.

Even smoke-abhorring church folks got paid in weed. As sexton of the Jones Hole Church in Virginia, SUSANNA WOODLIEF drew 400 pounds a year; down

65

the road a piece, at the less affluent Sappony Church, SARAH WILLIAMS got a modest 250 pounds of Virginia's best blonde per annum.

BED, BREAKFAST & BLACKSMITHING

Boston women have always had a stop-at-nothing attitude. Perhaps they got it from the likes of MARY SALMON, who inherited her late husband's forge and bellows in 1754. Soon she began running ads in the Boston *Evening Post*, assuring the horseshoe-hungry clientele that all was well: "Mary Salmon continues to carry on the business of horse-shoeing, as heretofore, where all gentlemen may have their Horses shod in the best Manner, as also all sorts of Blacksmith's Work done with Fidelity and Dispatch." Did Mary put the metal to the oatburners herself? Possible but not likely, given the other ads she ran for her boardinghouse, promising "to entertain boarders in a genteel manner". Since her late husband was rumored to have been poisoned, dining at Mary Salmon's — and the risks attendant — might have been part of the entertainment.

Another largely unsung Bostonian who liked a challenge was ELIZABETH HAGER, known as "Handy Betty the Blacksmith" for her skill with red-hot metals. Handy Betty did more than reshoe horses. During the Revolutionary War years, her ability to repair broken guns and muskets, to say nothing of the odd cannon captured from the Redcoats, made her invaluable.

During the 1700s, you could find female blacksmiths in many of the colonies. Often they were women like

JANE BURGESS of Maryland, who'd pitched in to help her husband while he was alive, and found herself the sole smith after his death in 1773. Was there consumer resistance to females doing such undainty labor? Heck no. In fact, the shortage of labor in this pre-industrial period meant that blacksmiths and other workers, whatever their gender, usually got equal pay.

MOM-AND-DAUGHTER VOODOO

For three-quarters of a century, an artful woman named MARIE LAVEAU was one of the hottest tickets in New Orleans. A superb cook and a hairdresser, the art for which she became famous locally had a darker hue. Marie was a voodoo queen.

Born free in 1794 in the French colony then called Saint-Dominique (part of Haiti today) Marie fled to New Orleans after that island's bloody slave uprising. A café au lait beauty, she married another refugee, a free black named Jacques Paris. Together they had some fifteen children, including her lookalike daughter, Marie.

With all those mouths to feed, Marie took her culinary and coiffure skills to a place with a huge captive audience: the New Orleans city jail. Scoff if you like — granted, the tips weren't all that great. And the ambiance? Fuhgeddaboutit. No *bons temps* rolling at all.

But Marie schmoozed as she cooked and combed, filing away off-the-record confidences and dirty linen dope on locals from white politicos to black debutantes, learning whose skeletons were in what closet, and so on. That data bank became her key to business success when Marie started her own voodoo hotline. (First, however, she took night classes with New Orleans legend Dr. John, whose excellent spy system she emulated.)

For decades, people came to high priestess Laveau seeking love charms, clairvoyant readings about future enterprises, and treatment of physical ailments. Celebrities, society women, ambitious politicians all knocked on her door on St. Ann Street. Marie didn't ignore the "little people", either. Even slaves showed up, seeking "secret" guidance for escape attempts! (Poor folks got dinged a mere 10 bucks per visit, while the sliding scale went up-up-up for the well heeled.)

At that time, there were more than 300 voodoo practitioners in the city, but only Marie was called the Boss Woman. On Bayou St. John she held standing-room-only rituals, the most famous of which took place on June 24 each year. Her show-stopping program included beheading live roosters and dirty dancing with Zombi, her ten-foot-long snake.

In later years, Marie got a little bored with pure voodoo (simulated public sex and drinking chicken blood gets really old, y'know?), and started sticking Catholic touches, from holy water to incense, into her shtick. By the time she took up residence in her fetish-decorated tomb in 1881, The *New Orleans Picayune* newspaper eulogized, "All in all, Marie Laveau was a wonderful woman. She died with a firm trust in heaven".

As canny as her mother, daughter Marie Laveau took up data mining and voodoodom where La Laveau left off, and accumulated even more power and wealth.

BRAZEN HUSSY SELLS HEAVY METAL

Four years after her marriage to one man, free spirit MARY JACKSON went into the hardware business with another. (Her everlovin' may have kicked the bucket by then, of course.) Her partner, Robert Charles, traveled to London to buy ironmongery, nails, cutlery, brass items, pewter, and lead. Lots of lead. But before the partners even got the doors open, they had a falling out.

A year later, on her own, Mary opened the Brazen Head. While selling hardware and heavy metals, she kept her eye on consumer trends. Shrewdly noting the healthy death rate in colonial Boston, she imported and sold mourning clothes. Later came her specials on dishes made of pewter, lead, and shot. (Unwittingly, her dishes may have helped the untimely death rate reach record levels.)

In 1750, the hardware maven began to explore her own creativity, announcing to the world in a print ad that "the said Mary makes and sells Tea-Kettles and Coffee-Pots, copper Drinking-Pots, brass Sauce-Pans, Fish-Kettles, &".

It was easy to sell things in Jackson's time; easier, mind you, than getting paid for them. As other merchants did, Jackson asked for cash but also took "truck that will answer" (that is, useable barter). By 1759, her son William was old enough to become her partner. Despite a fire that destroyed their shop, the two kept the Brazen Head going, now selling pork, butter, and olive oil from Florence. At some point, Mary let her son take charge of moving the margarine and the cutlery, giving herself a few years of discounted meals and senior leisure before her death around 1780.

NO MARTYR IN THIS FAMILY

LEONA VICARIO, only child of rich parents from Spain, didn't need to moonlight as a spy (code name: "Little Henrietta"), or finance a Mexican rebellion — she just wanted to. Born in Mexico in 1789, she exemplified the philosophical longing of her time: "Cut us loose from the royals already!"

Leona got many of her high-falutin' ideas from her unusual mother, Camila, who insisted on a liberal education in politics, history, and the arts. At eighteen, the girl got a hard knock: her folks died within months of each other. Then Mexico's war for independence broke out. Faster than the Concorde, her fiancé, a slick young lawyer, hightailed it for Spain. Sensing her engagement was off, Vicario began her own independence movement. Although he was a royalist fan, her guardian, Uncle Pomposo, proved a pushover; soon she had her own house and servants in another part of Mexico City, where she began spy-in-training work.

"Little Henrietta" directed a private mail service, encoded for security, between patriots in the capital and rebel forces outside it. She also rounded up a corps of armorers and set them up at a secret base, where their abilities kept the rebel guns firing. Over time, unbeknownst to Pomposo, she pumped pesos in the high six figures into the war effort.

With her high profile, Leona caught some prison time. After she spent forty-two days in interrogation in 1813, her comrades finally broke into the facility and extracted her, disguised as a mule skinner in blackface. The ruse worked. Leona, now armed with paper and ink (with which she fired "weapons of thought"), made her way to the rebel camp where General Morelos was in command.

In mid-revolution, young love hit. Leona met Andrés Quintana Roo, another sleek Spanish lawyer. This one, however, was a rebel sympathizer. The lovebirds honeymooned on the lam and soon were fugitives. Cheerily ignoring the downswing of the war, Leona and Andrés nursed the wounded, gave fiery speeches, and kept donating funds for years. In January 1817, Leona gave birth in a cave to a brand-new baby rebel named Genoveva.

After another year of running, they were captured, baby and all. Several offers, counteroffers, and other maneuvers later, the little family obtained its freedom. Well, sort of. The Roos were confined to the small town of Toluca, forbidden to work, and were under constant surveillance.

Eventually the rebels prevailed, and Mexico was free. In 1823, Leona and Andrés got a "surviving patriots award": honors, political position, and three houses to live in. Delighted to take up the role of housewife, Leona lived to be fifty-three, and was called "the glory of her country" to the end.

BAD AS I WANNA BE

Frankly, life could be dull around the tavern that LUCRETIA CANNON ran in little old Reliance, Delaware. A bit of crime to liven things up and make some serious coin — that was the ticket. So Lucretia, called "Patty" by everyone — at least, those who survived — set up a nifty organized crime ring.

It was the 1820s, and demand for black slaves was beginning to skyrocket in the southern states. There weren't many folks in bondage around Reliance — most of its African American citizens were free. Patty could fix that. She set her gang to kidnapping free blacks, then conducted a brisk under-the-table business to sell her live merchandise to slave traders. Her job was made much easier by the prodigious quantities of rum, gin, and beer consumed by everyone.

Like her tavern, the crime biz had its ups and downs. As Patty found, in organized crime, you don't fire people — you bury them. Leading by example, Cannon personally rubbed out eleven victims. At one point, she even had to add her own too-chatty husband to the statistics.

Our loose Cannon's crime ring and juke joint sailed along until 1829, when the law caught and convicted Lucretia. Rather than face up to her felonies, Cannon finagled a rope and took herself out of this world before the state of Delaware could beat her to it.

CHAPTER
THREE

Chain Breakers & Rebellion Makers

SHADES OF GRAY

Things weren't always black or white in the complex history of American slavery. Take ELIZABETH KEY. She was born to an unnamed slave around 1635. The father was Thomas Key, a white fellow who'd gotten her mother with child — and been slapped with a fine for doing so. Feeling guilty, Key sought to improve his daughter's legal status by getting her christened; then he roped in one Colonel Higginson to act as the baby's godfather. Nice move.

Oh, wait. Having second thoughts about his charity, the new dad now sells baby Elizabeth to the Colonel! "But only for nine years," Key vowed, adding, "and I made him promise to use her more respectfully than a common servant or slave." What a comfort.

By 1654, Elizabeth was nineteen and savvy enough to appeal to the Virginia courts. She'd put in her nine years with Higginson, plus more time with another master. Finding an attorney to file a petition, she asked the courts to grant her freedom.

Hallelujah — the court saw things her way! Besides freeing her, they recommended that Miss Key's master give her "Corne and Cloathes . . . and satisfaction (back pay, perhaps?) for the time she hath served longer than Shee ought to have done . . ."

After this splendid closure, Elizabeth turned to personal matters. She and her lawyer, William Greensted, were married on July 21, 1656 — the day the court decision came down. A love match? Pure pragmatism? We'll never know.

Soon after, the state of Virginia passed two pieces of legislation. The first forbade interracial marriage; the second made all mulattos slaves for life. Future children of interracial unions would not be as lucky as Elizabeth Key.

RIOT GRRRLS IN OLD VIRGINIA

In 1676, a strange coalition formed in Virginia Colony: settlers ticked off about the sharp increase in Indian raids, women who thought the Brits' lack of support sucked, and slaves, who had plenty of issues. Nearly twenty members of this group, called "Bacon's Rebellion", had their property confiscated and were hanged by the Virginia governor for such inflammatory activities as burning down Jamestown. Even so, a handful of vociferous "Bacon babes" kept up the good fight. Some, like SARAH DRUMMOND and LYDIA CHIESMAN, speechified about the villainy of England. Taking her case clear to the Mother Country, Sarah eventually got her own property restored — a grandiose gesture that made her almost overlook her husband's recent execution.

Writer ANNE COTTON chronicled the rebellion. In her book, ringleader Nathaniel Bacon came off in a rather poor light; Cotton was obliged to point out that on at least one occasion, he'd used four women as a body shield!

OF HUMAN BONDAGE

Housemaid CATHERINE DOUGLAS was mighty miffed. In 1696, she'd signed on as an indentured servant for four years to a guy named Mottrom Wright. Well, she'd mopped nonstop until 1700 — then her master pulled a fast one, claiming she'd signed a seven-year agreement. (He'd taken the precaution of destroying the original contract.) Catherine didn't buy it. "Wright is wrong, wrong, wrong!" she proclaimed, and took Mottrom to court. Normally servants were at a disadvantage in legal matters. Catherine, however, put together an excellent case. She found an attorney and rounded up three witnesses who swore they'd seen Douglas' contract — and it definitely said four, not seven years. A smack of the gavel, and it was all over. "The plaintiff wins," said the judge, and Catherine Douglas walked out of a Virginia courtroom, free and unemployed.

NANNY GOT THEIR GOAT

Shanghaied, kicking and screaming, from an African tribe called the Aka and taken on a slave ship to Jamaica, GRANDY NANNY was not your average slave. Or your average woman, either, as the ruling English painfully found out.

An obeah woman, or priestess in secret African practices, she was an adept in magic and herbs who could scare the bejesus out of almost anyone. Grandy Nanny consulted privately on matters from love potions to poisoning that certain obnoxious someone. She led group dances and ecstatic ceremonies of obeah worship. That made her powerful spiritually and politically.

As she grew older, she became a leader of the Windward Maroons, one of several large groups of runaway slaves that inhabited the lush, mountainous interior of Jamaica. Before and after Nanny's day, thousands of Maroons formed independent "nations" on the island and other places around the Caribbean, and were perennial thorns in the sides of would-be white colonizers.

In 1739, Nanny and others fired up the Windward Maroons to attack the whites. (The Leeward Maroons had just signed a peace treaty, after thirteen years of fighting.) For a while, the Redcoats didn't get it: How could an old sorcerer — and a woman, to boot — possibly be the rebels' leader?

80

When the British army began a personal Nanny-hunt, she set up her headquarters in the highest reaches of the Blue Mountains. The wilderness lent itself well to guerrilla activity. With her war chief, Nanny rallied her machete-armed troops, fomented riots among locals, and fought the "red ants," as she called them, until they finally tired of the whole bloody show and signed a peace accord.

Maroons continued to live in their free societies, and ably defend them, until the end of the eighteenth century. Even now, inhabitants of places like Moore Town and Nanny Town proudly claim to be descendants of Grandy Nanny, one of Jamaica's six national heroes. Since 1993, archaeological teams sponsored by Earthwatch have been excavating Nanny Town, named for the never-say-quit warrior sorceress.

FIERY WOMEN TAKE ENGLISH IN TWO

If you lived in old Nicaragua, and your name was Rafaela Herrera, you had a better-than-average chance of being a heroine. An impossible dream? Historical synchronicity? You decide.

In 1762, a nineteen-year-old named RAFAELA HERRERA DE URDIATE was moping around her dad's command post, the castle fortress of La Purísima Concepción. Nothing to do. Not a shopping mall in sight. *Nada*. Suddenly, up the San Juan River came a flotilla of fifty mean-looking vessels, bristling with cannons, and attacked.

As the ships fire on the castle, Rafaela's pop has his own attack of something — and drops dead at her feet. Now Rafaela is really worked up. Yelling "I can do this!" she assumes command. The first report she gets says that the attackers are English ships, loaded with Carib Indian troops. The second says No, they're English pirates, come to sack the city of Granada. Rafaela says, "Whatever."

For five days and nights, Rafaela mounts a keen defense and offense. Then — lucky break — her side manages to kill the enemy fleet's commander. Inexplicably, the fleet lingers, until Herrera heroically devises a new strategy. She hands out chunks of cloth, instructing her forces to set them ablaze and let them drift on the water, once it's totally dark. When the

English (well known for being phobic about fabric fires) spot the eerily burning phantom fleet, they're gone.

Two years later, another RAFAELA HERRERA (this one's moniker includes "y Sotomayor") grabs a heroine's medal for defending another castle fortress in Nicaragua. The darned English are trying to invade again; Spain's at war with England, meaning poor little Nicaragua is also. A more seasoned married woman, this Rafaela runs a red-hot cannon from the walls of the Castillo de San Juan. For her efforts, the king of Spain awards her a pension, an inheritance, and some property — but not, we hope, one of those oh-so-attackable castle fortresses.

In today's Nicaragua, the name "Rafaela Herrera" is still revered by poets and public alike, and is plastered on everything from schools to neighborhoods.

HOT WATER SPECIALIST

Lest we forget: Women fought on both sides of the wars on early American soil. Not all the aggression was aimed at the enemy, either. MARTHA MAY, for instance, got into a brawl with her soldier husband, then mouthed off at his colonel. That's how the pair found themselves in a British lockup in Carlisle, Pennsylvania. In due time, Private May got released — but his wife didn't. Martha, however, an army wife with twenty-two years' time in grade, knew how to grovel. In short order, she dashed off an apology to the colonel, saying, "I've traveld with my Husband every Place or Country the Company marcht too, and have workt very hard ever since I was in the Army. I hope yr Honour will be so good as to Pardon me this onct time that I may go with my Poor Husband one time more, to carry him and my good Officers water in ye Hottest Battle as I have done before. Yr unfortunate Petitioner and Humble Servant, Martha May." From the slim evidence of this delightful letter, maybe Martha managed to keep out of ye Hottest Water from then on.

DEAD WOMAN RIDING

Few know that a slave woman known only as LUCY took part in the famous Nat Turner Rebellion of 1831. The rebellion itself, the slaughter of forty-five Virginia whites during a forty-eight-hour period, was carried out by a handful of men. Inspired, like other slaves in the area, by the actions of Turner's band, Lucy turned on her own household at the plantation of John T. Barrow. She grabbed a white woman and held her hostage. Right away, Lucy fell out of favor with the rebels. They wanted to execute her hostage; Lucy did not. These niceties didn't matter a whit to vengeful white Southerners, who eventually captured every slave who had been involved in the insurrection. Like the others, Lucy was sentenced to be hanged. No words of contrition from her — instead, this clear-eyed slave made a powerful statement by riding to her execution sitting atop her own coffin.

WOULDN'T BE PRUDENT; DID IT ANYWAY

A soft-spoken Quaker from rural Rhode Island, PRUDENCE CRANDALL started her own female academy in Canterbury, Connecticut, in 1833. It soon became a fashionable place to send young women. Young white women, that is.

Canterbury was an all-Caucasian community, and Prudence's white skin fit right in. But local faces started turning beet red when SARAH HARRIS, a gifted young black woman, applied to the school, saying, "I want to get more learning, if possible enough to teach colored children. If you will admit me to your school, I shall forever be under greatest obligation to you." After due consideration, Crandall admitted her.

With head-swimming speed, whites yanked their daughters out, until none were left. Crandall calmly countered by reopening her school for blacks only. She got pupils by advertising her academy in the Boston and New York papers, helped by abolitionists in those cities.

Her act of courage brought down a firestorm. Locals threw manure in her well and rotting carcasses on her property. The school was physically attacked by angry mobs, and Crandall had to move classes for safety's sake. No one would sell Prudence any supplies, not even a stinking cabbage.

In 1834, the Connecticut legislature passed the shameful Black Laws, prohibiting the establishment of any school for nonresident blacks without local consent. Crandall was arrested and convicted for refusing to comply with the law. Soon after, a Court of Appeals reversed the decision, and released her on a technicality.

The despicable behavior of townspeople and legislature failed to get the better of Prudence. She struggled on until September 9, 1834, when her house was trashed and her school burned to the ground. Local officials turned a blind eye, while she and her pupils had to flee. Not a pretty moment for the state of Connecticut.

Somehow, amidst all this brouhaha, Prudence met and married a preacher named Philleo. Surveying the barbecued ruins of her academy, the two decided the only option left was to move. Moving "out West" to Kansas, the Philleos lived unremarked until the 1880s — when his death, and her poverty, came to the tardy attention of the town of Canterbury. A guilt-steeped group of citizens petitioned the legislature to give Prudence a pension, expunge her "criminal" record, and restore her good name. (And theirs, in the process.)

Author Mark Twain even offered to kick in some money so the eighty-two-year-old could return to Canterbury — to which Prudence hastily responded, "Thanks (no way in hell) but no thanks." After another round of feel-good petitions and news coverage,

Prudence herself wrote, "When your telegram (announcing legislative granting of a pension) arrived, the only jubilant display I wished to make was ... for the change that has been wrought in the views and feelings of the people."

MARK YOUR CALENDARS

No American — least of all BIDDY MASON herself — ever had a national holiday on November 16. Nevertheless, in 1989, the city of Los Angeles officially declared it "Biddy Mason Day", honoring her with a memorial at the Broadway Spring Center with a ceremony attended by the mayor and thousands of well-wishers. Who was this unknown honoree?

Born in 1818 on a Mississippi plantation, Bridget Mason was owned by Rebecca and Robert Smith — and exploited sexually by Big Daddy Robert. She had three daughters, all said to be his. Biddy was twenty-nine when her owner became a Mormon: "Okay — now we're moving out West!" On the trip, Biddy got a chance to develop her talents for cattle herding, midwifery, and mass cookery.

First stop, Utah. A few years later, they moved to southern California, so the Smiths could join the Brigham Young Mormon sect that believed in hot tubs.

Smith soon got a major revelation — from the lips of Biddy, who by now had met a free black or two and learned that slavery was illegal in the Golden State. She petitioned the court for her freedom. Hastily, Smith tried to move all his slaves to Texas, but the court found in Biddy's favor. With a cheery, *"Hasta la vista*, honky!" Mason headed for L.A. and a paying job as a nurse-midwife.

It took this hard-working, frugal woman a decade to buy her first piece of Los Angeles real estate, which made her one of the first black women to own land there. After that, Biddy parlayed her business acumen and her thrift into a fortune — which she largely spent on charity, from feeding the poor to founding the First African Methodist Episcopal, the area's first black church.

SAY IT OUT LOUD . . .

We've forgotten — or never learned about — half the work done in the past against racism. More than 150 years ago, for instance, this country had a vice president with a major closet skeleton. Richard Mentor Johnson freely opened that closet to acknowledge two out-of-wedlock daughters, sired with a woman of color. The kids in question? IMOGENE and ADALINE JOHNSON, his pert daughters. In 1836, Democrat Johnson was elected vice president, along with President Martin Van Buren, and served his 1837-1841 term. Aside from some cartoons, not much political hay was made of the Johnson sisters.

Right about then, politicos and public alike had their hands full with a far more impertinent pair of sisters: ANGELINA and SARAH GRIMKÉ. Born into a southern slave-holding family, these nice white girls matured into Quaker converts, abolition activists, and suffragettes in later life. Unlike Harriet Beecher Stowe, who cashed in on a growing distaste of slavery with *Uncle Tom's Cabin*, Angelina and Sarah were early advocates of immediate emancipation for blacks. Gutsy and vocal, Angelina and Sarah traveled (*sans* husbands — how vulgar!), published anti-slavery tracts, and lectured — even when the crowd hissed. Their convictions and courage rattled windows. And ultimately, hearts.

DREAM WEAVER

High human drama can be found on a scrap of paper. Take the single extant letter written by HANNAH HARRIS, a Virginia slave on plantation Leo, one of eighteen belonging to slaveholder-planter Robert Carter. Besides being literate, Hannah was a talented weaver. Her owner even rented out her flax-weaving skills.

For a man who held thousands of human beings as chattel, Carter wasn't a bad guy. Prodded by the enlightened laws passed by Virginia in 1782, after the Revolutionary War, or by conscience and his religious conversion from Baptism to the Swedenborgian America New Church, he began proceedings to free his slaves. Not all at once, you understand — that would be inconvenient. This was a timed release of 500 slaves over twenty-one years.

When 1792 rolled around, Hannah got the news. "Congrats! You'll be freed next January," her owner said. Thirty-seven-year-old Hannah sat down and wrote him a letter. A mushy "Thank you, massa" note, perhaps? Not a chance. Like others in human bondage, Hannah thought hard about her future. She asked Carter if she could buy back her own loom — to make a living once free. Was her request granted? Most probably. In the relatively "tolerant" years between 1782 and 1800, more than 10,000 slaves like Hannah Harris were freed in Virginia.

INDEPENDENCE — IT'S CONTAGIOUS

After subduing New World populations of Central and South America via bloodshed, fatal European diseases, Catholicism, and interracial dating, the conquerors from Spain were naturally reluctant to lose their treasures. One by one, however, the Latin American countries broke free.

Spain's most precious holding, Mexico, was the last. In 1810, Mexico began fighting its first war of independence, led by charismatic priest Miguel Hidalgo and a huge band of pitchfork-ready peasants.

At that time, GERTRUDIS BOCANEGRA was pushing forty and living a genteel life in the sweet lakeside suburbs of Pátzcuaro, Mexico. A privileged kid, she'd married an ensign in the royal army. Then she heard one of Hidalgo's "Let's build a republic" sound bites, and was won over. She strong-armed her husband and son into joining up as well: "So what if Junior is only ten — it'll be a learning experience!"

A born organizer, Gertrudis rounded up supplies for the rebel forces, mustered a female army, signed up her own daughters, acted as spy and go-fer, and saw action on the front with female companions.

Despite Gertrudis's best efforts, Hidalgo's poorly trained troops started losing decisive battles. By the summer of 1811, Hidalgo's head adorned the top of a pole. A bounty of 50 to 500 pesos was offered for other rebel noggins, depending on rank.

Despite the headlessness of the independence movement, Gertrudis and others continued to fight for years. There were low moments — both her son and husband were killed. But Gertrudis finally got her most exciting mission: sent to spy in her home turf, she vacuumed up strategic info on the enemy, meanwhile trying to convince royalist troops to switch sides. Some bigmouth in town spotted her in action, though; Bocanegra and her two daughters were thrown into prison.

At that crossroad, Gertrudis could have saved her own skin by identifying other local sympathizers. This she refused to do. After a sham trial, she fearlessly faced a firing squad in the winter of 1818. Not until 1823 would the Mexican independence for which she gave her life be won.

BACK TO AFRICA — CHAPTER 1

MATILDA NEWPORT, a free black who'd lived most of her long life in the northeastern states, dreamed of Africa. Along with high-profile organizer Paul Cuffee and others, she left home to start a new nation of blacks. Beginning in 1815, ships like the *Traveler* and the *Nautilus* sailed to Sierra Leone and Liberia, filled with "Back to Africa" colonists — 125 from Maryland alone.

Matilda's group came in 1822. Once they arrived, the colonists paid a pittance for land in West Africa, building a compound with a stockade fence — a highly prudent move, since local tribes resented them terribly. Instead of bringing a "Welcome home" gift basket, they attacked with spears and arrows on December 1.

After much fighting, the locals were getting the best of the newcomers, when Matilda strolled out of the compound, smoking a pipe. She casually moved toward the large gray novelty (a cannon they'd brought from the states) that the West Africans had captured and were examining. Cruising past, Matilda dropped a live coal from her pipe into the powder chamber.

Seconds later, a *ka-boom!* deafened the invaders, who fled. Pipe-smoker Newport and her colony of former slaves had won white-man style — by pushing out locals. By 1847, the region became the republic of Liberia.

NANNY'S REVOLTING NEWS

When she wasn't working her guts out as a slave on a Barbados plantation, NANNY GRIGG indulged a secret vice: she read the newspaper. In 1815, she told the other slaves they were damned fools to work any longer. They'd all be freed by New Year; hadn't she read it in print? (Another tragic example of early supermarket journalism.) January came and went, but Grigg kept her convictions. "We'll fight for freedom," she said. "Maybe we'll set fires, like the other slaves did in their swell rebellion over in Saint Domingue."

As senior domestic on the Simmons estate, Nanny became part of an inner circle that included chief conspirator Bussa. The Barbados Rebellion was no spur-of-the-moment melee; when Nanny and company struck on April 16, they had 400 trained fighters. It wasn't enough. After defeat, another slave's confession put Nanny in the driver's seat of the rebellion — and on the death cart. To her credit, Nanny Grigg wasn't afraid to die trying.

SEVEN YEARS A FREEDOM FIGHTER

POLICARPA SALAVARRIETA was born in Guaduas, a South American town that had long been revolting. In the political sense, that is. Her family and her town both nursed the idea of an independent New Granada (today's Colombia).

During La Pola's teens, her country was a tempestuous place that locals called *la patria boba* — our idiotic homeland. Some wanted Napoleonic rule. Others favored a republic. Still others pushed for a drug cartel to run things (or maybe that came later).

Once the battle for independence had begun, La Pola found it easy to get jobs in the snooty households of the privileged. A wonder with the needle, she mended and sewed as a faithful "background" servant, while soaking up valuable data for espionage efforts.

As a freedom fighter, La Pola took bigger risks than most. One unusual achievement of hers was to forge a circle of sister collaborators. Some were aristocrats, like ANDREA RICAURTE, whose home was a base of operations for La Pola and company. Another keen collaborator was MARÍA DEL CARMEN DE GAITÁN, whose sons, daughter, and husband were military patriots too. Working as a team, La Pola and these women recruited soldiers, later moving men and materials for the resistance effort.

In 1817, La Pola was captured and sentenced to be shot. As she and eight others were positioned to receive a bullet in the back, she cried out to the crowd, "How different would be our fate today if you knew the price of liberty!" Two years later, Salavarrieta's homeland of Colombia would win its freedom from Spanish rule.

FEMALE HANDS IN INCA'S LAST STAND

Peru was the pits in the 1780s — unless you were a Spanish tribute collector, that is. Native Incas were sucked dry by rapacious overlords, who also made peasants do forced labor in the mines.

Although of Spanish blood, young MICAELA BASTIDAS came to love the Inca way — and her royally descended Inca hubby, José Tupac Amaru. (She also adored his velvet clothes and waist-length ringlets.) She and José were naturals to lead a rebellion against the Spanish.

Although she had three young sons underfoot, Micaela made an excellent organizer. Thanks largely to her, José's clandestine army numbered thousands of nicely inflamed rebels. On November 4, 1780, they struck, kidnapping an important official. After ransoming the quivering bureaucrat for firearms, they hanged the guy — a flashy if unjust move that got everyone's attention.

While José handled the day-to-day massacres, Micaela coordinated troops and secured strategic bridges and roads. This skinny warrior woman leaned on locals to supply ammunition and food. "And while you're at it," she'd bark, "supersize that order of coca leaves (the chewable Inca narcotic)."

Soon the rebels controlled nine provinces, eight parishes of Cuzco, and various cities. Micaela encouraged other fem rebels to channel their energies onto the battlefield. With her mentoring, several women held military command — including MARÍA ESQUIVEL and TOMASA TITU CONDEMAYTA. Peasant women also fought like maniacs, often armed merely with standard-issue rocks. As one Spanish officer fearfully noted, "I've never seen such obstinacy, or such a desperate defense . . ."

As 1781 arrived, rebel forces took Picchu, cutting off the city of Lima from the provincial capital of Cuzco. But this success was the high point. Over Micaela's protests, José hesitated before besieging Cuzco, giving the enemy time to arm. Dumb. Then he lifted the siege. Dumber. Spaniards swarmed out of the city; in a few months, they'd turned the war around and put out an APB for rebel leaders.

After a farcical trial, Micaela and the others went to their deaths — carried out in a creatively gruesome manner. Micaela was garroted with an iron collar, but her neck was so thin, it wouldn't work. The Spaniards ad libbed with a lasso; once she was dead, they cut out her tongue, chopped her into pieces, burned some parts, and put others on display. This may be where the word *overkill* originated. Notwithstanding, Micaela Bastidas is still revered in old Peru.

WE HAD A DREAM, TOO

In the early years of the nineteenth century, two young black women had the same dream. HENRIETTE DELILLE and JULIETTE GAUDIN were both free citizens of Louisiana; both had struggled to become Catholic nuns of the Ursuline teaching order. Now they wanted to set up a religious order for poor blacks in New Orleans — as an alternative to the prostitution and sad street life that so many women of color endured.

You'd think the Catholic Church would clap its hands at this humanitarian idea. You'd be wrong. They fought it vigorously. At first, Henriette tried to set up a branch of integrated Ursulines. A ringing "No way!" came from the parish. But these two had the persistence of Superglue. In 1826, they got the go-ahead to establish a blacks-only order of the Sisters of the Holy Family. Its target audience: the quadroons of New Orleans. Instead of becoming courtesans in the Big Easy, the nuns were encouraged to live in chastity — or failing that, to marry a respectable black guy.

Finally, in 1842, the pushy pair also got approval for an all-black Community of the Holy Family. The church grumped, "You can open a school for girls, and maybe a hospice for the sick, and an orphanage. But no lessons for slave kids — and don't even think about wearing your habits outside of the convent!"

101

INSPIRATIONAL SURNAME

When the industrial revolution began revolving in the United States, women became a key part of the labor force, especially in the textile industry. Owners loved it: pay 'em a pittance, provide abysmal conditions — females would acquiesce. Surprise: Sometimes they didn't. In 1828, and frequently thereafter, women from New Hampshire and other states began striking.

In Taunton, Massachusetts, sixty young women protesting a wage cut walked off the job, led by a twenty-year-old preacher named SALOME LINCOLN. Weaver Lincoln, who took on millwork so she could continue to preach, tried to keep her group united. With no support or strike fund, the workers caved in, returning to the job one by one. But Salome Lincoln held firm — an early, nearly forgotten Norma Rae in the centuries-long fight for a job that wouldn't kill you or exploit you.

LIBERATOR OF "THE LIBERATOR"

"Gentle, crazy woman" was merely one of the admiring remarks directed at MANUELA SÁENZ, this one from her lover, continent liberator Simón Bolívar.

Ecuadorian Manuela had that checkered past so beloved of soap operas: illegitimate, did time in a nunnery, had a runaway love affair, was pushed into marriage with a dull English doctor.

By 1819, the countries of Ecuador, Bolivia, Peru, Colombia, and Venezuela were hip-deep in revolution. Refusing to stick to matters marital, Manuela offered her skills — good brain, sharp tongue, guts, sex appeal — to The Movement. At a liberation parade in 1822, she got a look at Bolívar, the Man of the Year: a tubercular-thin, big-nosed guy with a long sad face. When he looked up, she threw him a laurel wreath. That night, they danced and romanced at the victory ball — the beginning of an eight-year passion.

Chucking what few social conventions she honored, Manuela flaunted their relationship; frequently apart, the couple wrote voluminously. Not that she had Simón's undivided attention: it's a wonder he got any battles won, given the stream of ladies he entertained.

Bolívar had a disturbing attitude toward women: he dug their support, loved their money, and cherished their organizing abilities, especially Manuela's. But when it came to women enjoying full rights of citizenship in the new republics, he was against it.

Love-myopic Manuela continued to carry out spy operations and accompany Bolívar's armies into battle. Before long, however, latino politics turned against Bolívar: he'd gotten too big for his pantalones.

Manuela's life became a nightmare. She intercepted a series of death plots and saved Simón's life at a masquerade ball. In 1825, she foiled more conspirators, who sword-whipped her so stingingly that she spent two weeks in bed. All her loyalty and help couldn't turn the political tide — nor save Bolívar's life. He died of tuberculosis (and defeat) in 1830.

At length, Manuela Sáenz was driven from Colombia and exiled to Jamaica. Eventually she opened a tobacco shop on the Peru-Ecuador border, where she grew old and plump, still feisty and full of tales of herself and the Liberator, whom she outlived by twenty-six years. At length, Ecuador and the rest of South America paid her homage — the most beautiful gesture being a poem by Nobel laureate Pablo Neruda.

ALSO A BRAZILIAN'S BEST FRIEND

Until her twenties, Francisca (called "Xica" for short) was one of a sea of hard-working slaves in Diamantina, a town in the Minas Gerais region of Brazil. In 1739, however, a new guy came to town, one João Fernandes de Oliveira from Portugal. Already well heeled, João had gotten a lock on the extraction of diamonds for the area from the king. The monopoly was okay. But then he actually found the rocks.

Where to fritter away that newfound wealth? Slaves, of course. Xica caught his eye. And lickety-split, other body parts as well. Quickly he freed his new fancy, and made XICA DA SILVA part of his wild ride to the top of the Brazilian heap.

Da Silva was into charitable works — but as Mom had always told her, it began at home. To rub her rich 'n' free status in everyone's noses, she began to buy the finest clothes, throw the most excellent parties, and wear the most outrageous diamonds ever seen in the New World or Old. She and João had twelve years of a whole lot of excess before Oliveira got the dreadful news: like a faulty Ford Pinto, he'd been recalled to the home factory. What an Amazon-sized downer.

Brazilians never begrudged Xica her big win or her free-spending ways. We know that João died a poor man in Portugal — but Xica's last chapters remain a mystery. To this day, however, her flamboyance lives on in Brazilian legend and on the silver screen, where a Carlo Diegues film about conspicuous consumption continues to motivate young bimbos and would-be Evitas.

CHAPTER
FOUR

Creative Boatrockers & Career Widows

HOW MANY MAÑANAS TILL WE GET THERE?

You think travel delays and missed connections are stressful today — try putting yourself in MENCIA CALDERÓN's *tacones*. A society señora from Sevilla, Spain, the widowed Mencia was asked in 1550, "How'd you like to head up a group of fifty young women, including your daughters, take a nice sea voyage over to the New World — some colony called Paraguay — and settle the place? We can give you the Founder's Special!" After accepting, Calderón and company got on board. But smooth sailing it wasn't. There were perfect storms. Imperfect storms. Shipwrecks. And Indian attacks — and they weren't even near dry land yet! A full *five years* later, Mencia and her stalwart if incredibly bedraggled voyagers wobbled ashore at Asunción, Paraguay's capital. Despite their deplorable grooming and near-carcinogenic tans, the women got a lot of excited attention. Mencia's daughters soon married and produced little Asunciónites. In the years to come, Calderón would see her stamina and good sense passed on to another generation. As the colony's First Grandmother, she could brag that among her grandkids were the Bishop of Tucumán and the founder of the University of Córdoba.

COFFINS WITH A SILVER LINING

Born poor, a Mexican of mixed Spanish and Indian blood, with no access to education of any kind, MENCIA PÉREZ DE ARAGÓN had an innate shrewdness and that all-important quality for success: longevity. Her first husband, a Basque innkeeper, popped off in 1578. Besides the lodgings, he left a mill, grazing land, and other real estate. Pretty pronto, Mencia found a new significant other, a rancher named Rodrigo Arias. Alas, by 1590, Mencia was wearing widow's weeds again. This time, she added Rodrigo's carting business to her portfolio. In between funerals, Mencia had started a shingle business, with a workforce of local Indians. Ultimately, this career widow became Huamantla's biggest employer, the richest woman in town — and a fiscal force throughout Tlaxcala province.

STOP THE PRESSES! I'M IN LABOR!

What a time to be pregnant, thought South Carolinian ELIZABETH TIMOTHY. This hardy Huguenot transplant from Holland already had six youngsters. Then she got the horrible news that her beloved spouse Lewis had been killed in an accident. Plus it was Christmas, she was broke, and she needed to run the family business herself if she and the kids wanted to eat.

With a huge sigh, Mrs. Timothy waddled into her print shop and set type for the upcoming issue: "Whereas the late Printer of this Gazette hath been deprived of his life by an unhappy Accident, I take this opportunity of informing the Publick, that I shall continue the Paper as usual, and hope by the assistance of my Friends to make it as entertaining and correct as may be reasonably expected. Wherefore I flatter myself, that all those Persons, who, by Subscriptions or otherwise, assisted my late Husband in the Prosecution of the said undertaking, will be kindly pleased to continue their Favours and good Offices to his poor afflicted widow with six small children and another hourly expected."

That "hourly expected" really got to them; subscriptions to the paper grew gratifyingly. Elizabeth's notice in the *South Carolina Gazette* appeared on January 11, 1739, making her the first female to run and edit a newspaper in that state. Her printing skills may have been learn-as-you-go, but her Dutch education and abilities as a trained accountant really helped.

After birthing her seventh child and her first tabloid, the unsinkable Timothy continued as a journalist and publisher for a decade, increasing the paper's circulation and publishing twice a week instead of once. Thanks to her fiscal moxie, she even bought out the paper's other investor — a certain Benjamin Franklin.

Eventually, her son Peter took over. Elizabeth, however, kept on working. In 1746, she used the *Gazette* to advertise her own enterprise next door, where she sold pocket Bibles, primers, hornbooks, and reflections on courtship and marriage.

Timothy women couldn't keep out of print, it seems. After Peter died, his widow ANN TIMOTHY became South Carolina's official state printer — while sidelining, like her mother-in-law, as a retailer of stationery supplies and women's accessories.

WIDOWS WHO LOVE BOZOS TOO MUCH

Named "Coosaponakeesa" in the early 1700s, she got the more mundane baptismal name of Mary after she was sent to school in South Carolina. At sixteen, she married an Alabama trader named John Musgrove. MARY MUSGROVE had an intellect as sharp as a Creek Indian hatchet, a weapon she also knew how to handle.

Thanks to her education and her trilingualism (she could speak Creek, English, *and* Alabaman), Mary played a leadership role in local race relations. When Savannah, Georgia, was settled by English philanthropist James Oglethorpe, Mary became his interpreter and chief liaison. He thought so highly of Mary, he actually *paid* her.

Mary's troubles began when her first mate bit the dust; she then wed Jacob Matthews, who just didn't hold up well, either. Finally she hooked up with a crooked clergyman named Tommy Bosomworth. With a name like that, you know he's going to be trouble. Mr. B was greedy — and just smart enough to see that manipulating Mary could get him money and perks. Bozo-needy Musgrove fell for his flattering daydreams: "Forget the white settlers — you'd make a fabulous queen of the Creeks!"

Accordingly, in 1749 Mary assembled her Creek warriors and yes-men, marched into Savannah in full war-bonnet mode, and scared the pea-wadding out of

112

its citizens. Mary and the warriors terrorized the place for a month, after which she rethought Tommy's notion, and ordered everyone to put away their scalping instruments.

Here and there, over the years, Mary had accumulated a lot of Georgia real estate. She'd also earned a salary of 100 pounds a year from Oglethorpe, who threw in a diamond ring and a cash bonus when he left for England. These worldly goods still weren't enough for Mr. Bosomworth, who pressed Mary for more funds.

At his instigation, the couple traveled to England, where Mary laid another invoice on the crown for services rendered. It took five years, but Mary finally received an incredible 2,100-pound bonus — plus ownership of St. Catherine's Island, off the Georgia coast. (Maybe Bosomworth's ideas weren't all bad.) Roomy enough for a mansion and Tommy's cattle-ranch fantasy, St. Catherine's was their small island in the sun until the much-married Musgrove went to a happier hunting ground in 1763.

An Embarrassment of Riches

Sure, an absentee husband meant she never had a man on hand for those pesky dike repairs. Nevertheless, MARIE VAN RENSSALAER would just as soon have stayed in her comfortable home in Holland. But in 1674, she got the news that her husband had thoughtlessly died, thousands of miles across the sea — which made it awfully hard to send flowers. The deceased, an administrator of the New Netherland colony in what would one day be New York, had left a big estate. Marie had to take it over. And she had to administer it *pro tem*.

"Good grief! Nobody told me it was the size of a European country!" was the widow's reaction, when she and her six youngsters wobbled off the ship. Her estate, called Renssalaerwyck, covered 700,000 acres and ran along both sides of the Hudson River, as far as she could see. The new colonist set to work.

Marie's daily to-do list was formidable: oversee the grist mill, oversee the sawmill, buy wheat, sell lumber, pay natives ridiculously small sums for fabulous furs, sell furs for fabulous prices to Dutch buyers . . . it was never-ending.

To add insult to injury, her brother-in-law in Holland sent a constant stream of "advice" and criticism — but never lifted an actual finger on either shore. At one point, a very ticked-off Marie wrote him, saying, "I've lost my health and my dearest partner, I'm saddled with six kids and an estate encumbered to the max. What about *my* needs??"

The widow toughed it out for nearly two decades. What with New Netherland changing from Dutch hands to British, it took until 1685 just to get clear title to her lands. Finally, however, her oldest son reached puberty, and she could drop the administration of the estate on his shoulders — at which point this good woman kicked back for a well-earned rest, and a nip of good schnapps, perhaps. Let someone else underpay the natives and overcharge the Dutch for a while.

DOCTOR FEES — JUST DON'T INHALE

During the blithely unregulated period before the Revolutionary War, DR. KATHY HEBDEN whacked off limbs, administered various nasty nostrums, and bled 'em with the best of 'em. (And she wasn't the only female sawbones around.)

No doubt her Maryland patients were grateful. The problem was compensation. In order to collect, Hebden had to sue as often as she sutured. She even dragged her carpenter husband Tom into the collection side of the business. During the 1640s, she and her husband became familiar faces at the provincial court.

First was that deadbeat, Edward Hall. After doing leg surgery and "dieting him" for seven weeks, Kathy received 10 percent of the agreed-upon fee. Into court they went, and won their claim.

Two years down the road, Dr. H cured another fellow of ague and fever, purged him, and bled him. Upon nonpayment, she strode into the courthouse for another victory. Then followed a successful suit against George Manners for medicine, and a whopping big settlement for doctoring Richard Lawrence.

At that time, doctors weren't paid in money; like many other businesspeople in the American colonies, they received tobacco as legal tender. So what Dr. Kathy collected was a small mountain of nicotine.

116

(Toxic pay indeed; but then, the medical treatments and nostrums of the day probably weren't much better.)

CHALK UP ANOTHER FIRST

HENRIETTA DEERING JOHNSTON: yet another artist whose life and reputation have disappeared into the historical murk. Born in Dublin, Ireland, she married a poor preacher (two strikes against her already). The Johnstons emigrated to America and settled in Charleston, South Carolina, where they proceeded to have five children.

Though literate and kind, Mr. J was a disaster as a provider. Henrietta had to augment the family income by doing portraits of Charleston's vain and well heeled. In 1716, more disaster struck: the preacher drowned in the harbor, leaving Henrietta to tread water, financially speaking. Now she needed to produce art just to survive.

Her specialty — working in newfangled pastel chalks — had been pioneered by the talented Italian Rosalba Carriera. Henrietta was a great reader; that may be how she came to know Carriera's works. There remain no clues as to how this indomitable talent got her professional training — if indeed she did.

Between 1716 and her death near sixty, Henrietta created more than forty portraits; perhaps the most famous is a haunting portrait of Thomas Moore as a child.

THAR SHE BLOWS!

Her man, Colonel William Smith, had just turned up his toes. What was MARTHA TURNSTALL SMITH to do? After an interval of mourning, she followed the desire she'd nursed in her breast for years — widow Smith became a whaler. Living as she did on Long Island, she established her own whaling company out of St. George's Manor. A keen businesswoman with account-ing savvy (and a strong stomach — ever gotten a whiff of whale blubber?), Martha launched her operation in January 1707.

Her handwritten records report bonanza days like February 24, when "my company killed a school whale, which made 35 barrels [of oil]." Environmental concerns didn't cross the mind of this nautical dowager. That year, her company whacked out a number of yearling whales. Martha even noted the slaughter of something she called a "stunt whale". (Too bad Sea World wasn't up and running — Smith could have been sitting on a cetacean gold mine.)

In her first year, Smith did so well that she had to pay substantial duties on the oil, proving once again that, even on dry land, there's always a whale of a price to pay.

CLEARLY A BUBBLY NEW WORLD

Usually it was the wife who died after childbirth. In the case of Frenchwoman NICOLE-BARBE CLICQUOT, she and her baby girl survived, and her husband *c'était fini*. Married just three years, the twenty-year-old donned mourning clothes and adopted the funereal handle of *La Veuve Clicquot* (the widow of Clicquot). Oh well, black was always chic. And *très* slimming.

Daughter of the mayor of Reims, Nicole had gotten interested in vineyards and the making of champagne when she wed her shortlived winemaker in 1799. Now, under her own steam, she started hands-on experimentation. At that time, the addition of sugar and yeast to make champagne produced a beverage that was sludgy rather than scintillating. One day, Nicole had an ingenious idea: Why not store the bottles upside-down while they aged, to see if the sludge would work its way into the neck? She fooled around with giving the bottles a quarter-turn over the months. After a lot of messy experimentation (you shoulda seen that winery floor) she pioneered a way to whip out the cork, expel the sediment, and recork without losing the liquid.

After tasting her new clear-as-a-bell champagne, the young widow cried, "*Formidable — vive la Veuve!*" while her competitors slapped their foreheads in why-didn't-I think-of-that gestures, and gloomily drank all her samples.

120

By 1814, the tedious wars that France had been fighting — first with the British and then with their own Napoleon — came to an end. Clicquot's business shot ahead like a well-aimed champagne cork, leaving her more sedimentary competitors a distant second, third, fourth . . . (One of her better customers was former Empress Josephine, who ran up such a tab that it became a hot-button item in her divorce from Bonaparte.)

Not one to sit on her laurels, Nicole triumphed again with pink champagne. At age forty-three, Madame was able to retire to her chateau de Boursault in Boursin, living to a hearty eighty-nine, and still getting her daily exercise from lifting a glass of bubbly.

Perhaps even more than their French counterparts, women in America appreciated Nicole's breakthrough. At that time, the United States was awash in rum, beer, gin, whiskey, and other non-genteel drinks. Not a romantic bubble in the bunch.

When Clicquot came up with her winning way of making see-through champagne, she soon won a devoted new following across the Atlantic — including me. (I say: Why be a writer, if you can't slip in a vote for one or two of your favorite vices?)

WAXY BUILDUP

What's real fame? When your name becomes generic, like *sandwich* or *guillotine*. MARIE TUSSAUD achieved it; her name is synonymous with "wax head", as in Madame Tussaud's Wax Museum, begun in London in 1802.

Oddly enough, Marie's story involves guillotines as well. For years, she'd doodled around, modeling wax heads, taught by her uncle J. C., who owned a museum of the things. Eventually she got a part-time job as art tutor to the king of France's sister. You'd think it would add cachet to be a royal hanger-on. But when the French Reign of Terror began in 1793, Marie got introduced to a dungeon, imprisoned without even so much as a chunk of Play-Doh.

Things looked grim. Then: *le* breakthrough! While heads were rolling from the guillotine disassembly line, Marie got hired to make death masks from the freshly severed noggins. Mind you, it wasn't the best job in the world. Some of those severed heads had belonged to her friends.

But Marie gritted her teeth and persisted, producing a frightful array of wax portraits of the famous and infamous departed, including Marie Antoinette. Once the French Terror had subsided, Tussaud (who'd inherited the family collection) moved to London with her family in 1802, so that her heads could find a good home. Ghoulish Londoners went mad for Madame Tussaud's Exhibition, especially its Chamber of Horrors, a stroke of marketing genius. She soon had to move to a bigger location on Baker Street.

Later, she took her head shop on the road, touring the British Isles with her gallery of rogues, royals, and red-hot celebrities. Such was the demand that Madame Tussaud stayed on the circuit for thirty-three years.

After her demise at nearly ninety, fire destroyed Tussaud's building (and most of the earlier French wax heads) in 1925. Three years later, it reopened to the fascination and acclaim it continues to have today — and spawned a plethora of sincere if unflattering imitations, especially in the United States. Ironically, it was the heady success of PATIENCE WRIGHT, Tussaud's American contemporary and fierce competitor, that helped make Marie's "wax museum" into an international icon.

LOTS OF FUN, BUT ROYALTIES . . . NUN

Living in a Catholic nunnery like the Hotel Dieu convent in Montreal could be hell. But MARIA MONK had the real goods on the place. Prankish Monk knocked out detail after ghastly detail of her sojourn in a book whose title was almost longer than the text: *The Awful Disclosures of Maria Monk, as Exhibited in a Narrative of Her Sufferings during a Residence of Five Years as a Novice, and Two Years as a Black Nun, in the Hotel Dieu Nunnery at Montreal.*

Maria's effort — essentially fiction — was based on her seven-year stay at the convent, between intervals of active prostitution. She'd been urged to crank out her tell-all by a couple of anti-Catholic "publishers". They saw a tawdry opportunity for a book trashing Catholicism, which was suffering a backlash just then, thanks to the tidal wave of poor Catholic immigrants arriving in the New World from Ireland and France. Despite being made up, the book had an enormous impact. The post-pub aftermath, however, was a disaster every writer can relate to: instead of collecting royalties from eventual sales of 300,000 copies, Maria got taken to the cleaners. Disgusted, the perpetrator of the best literary hoax of her century went back to hooking — the only crooked game in which she knew the rules and controlled the cash flow.

VALET PARKING, HUMAN DOOR PRIZES

Thanks to Virginia's bumper crop of widows, Williamsburg in the 1700s had a social scene and then some. Competitive didn't half describe it. One particular pair went at it more intensely than Microsoft and Apple. WIDOW STAGG fired the first shot, advertising fancy dancing lessons in the local newspaper. WIDOW DEGRAFFENREIDT countered with the same offer. Then Stagg offered a private ball at her house, followed by an assembly. Her social counterpart followed suit. By 1738, at her next fete, Mrs. Stagg promised a raffle that included a male slave among the prizes! In addition, attendees would see "several grotesque dances never yet performed in Virginia". Grinding her teeth, her rival racked her brain and strained her inheritance to come up with her next social event. At *her* next ball, a lucky guest with the winning ticket would take home "a likely young Negro woman and her child". With door prizes like these, small wonder that slavery became a growth industry in Virginia.

THE MUSE — IT'S CATCHING

In this Philadelphia family, three sisters caught the muse — but SARAH MIRIAM PEALE got a chronic case. Maybe she excelled because she was the one Peale female who *didn't* get married.

Daughter of painter James Peale, niece of another artist, Sarah was born in 1800. With her sisters, she began studying at Dad's knee. He taught them the art of painting miniature portraits on ivory. Cute, but not quite the medium Sarah wanted to work in. She craved canvas. And got it. At seventeen, she exhibited her first paintings at the Pennsylvania Academy of the Fine Arts, and later moved to Baltimore to study with her uncle Charles Wilson Peale. Even as a teen, Sarah's way with textures and flesh tones was superb. Clientele and commissions for life-sized portraits in oils poured in the door of her studio.

Over the next twenty years, Sarah Miriam Peale completed more than 100 stunning portraits — from the glitterati of Baltimore to the political movers and shakers in Washington, D.C. The biggest name she captured on canvas was war hero General Lafayette. Sarah painted a superb likeness, but more than that, her realistic paintings had spiritual depth.

Eventually she tired of Baltimore and moved to St. Louis, where she turned out portraits and still-lifes for another three decades. At seventy-eight, still mad for canvas and with no Social Security in sight, she returned to Philly and the company of her sisters, where she stayed until her death at eighty-five.

Meanwhile, her older sister ANNA married a Claypole — yet another artistic family — and started her own dynasty. She was content to be a miniaturist, and a very good one she was. In fact, in 1824 she and Sarah had the dual honor of becoming Academicians at the Pennsylvania Academy of Fine Arts — its only two female members.

That third sister MARGARETTA? Cherished yet overshadowed by her siblings, her talent became an also-ran to her marriage into the Angelica family.

WRIGHT STUFF FOR HER TIMES

In the early 1700s, when Pennsylvania was "the new frontier", SUSANNA WRIGHT helped tame it. Where Susanna differed from other energetic, literate female Quakers of her zip code was in her marital status. Single — for eighty-seven years. This nearly unheard-of state of affairs was made even more galling by the fact that Susanna thrived on her status, grievously manless though it was.

The only male in sight was her doctor dad, a widower whose large household she managed. Educated in England, Miss Wright had far-flung interests. By turns bookworm, poet, letter writer, linguist, and bibliophile, she compiled one of the biggest libraries in the state, with volumes in Italian, Latin, and French, all of which she could read.

A naturalist at heart, Susanna read extensively in the field. She was keen on cultivating silkworms in Lancaster, and succeeded. Not content with these accomplishments, Susanna Wright made substantial contributions to her community, too. Although she didn't have a medical degree (few women did), Wright studied with her father and acted on various occasions as a physician.

The most valuable service this nonstop altruist may have rendered was in legal matters. Miss Wright often did *pro bono* work for those around her. She could draw

128

up a will or settle a property dispute with as much skill as she could write a poem, paint a picture, or pen a letter. Who says there were no Renaissance women in early America?

HURRICANE SUSANNA

The first few chapters of SUSANNA HASWELL's life were dismal. Born in Plymouth, England, in 1762, she lost her mother a few years later and emigrated with her dad to Boston, Massachusetts, where he became, tragically, . . . a tax collector. Anti-Brit feelings were running high, and it wasn't long before her dad got arrested, then held for three years without a trial. Meanwhile, the girl child kept house, whipping up a little toast for nourishment now and then, while delving in the works of Shakespeare and Homer.

In 1778 her dad was released, to the chorus of, "Thanks for visiting Massachusetts! Since you won't be using your property, we've confiscated it. Happy voyage back to England!"

At sixteen, Susanna took up governessing in England. While her charges snored, she worked on her first novel, called *Victoria*. Although you'd think she already had enough potboiler raw material, sweet Sue married Bill Rowson, a drunken party boy who provided her with enough anecdotes (but never income) for a lifetime.

Her second novel, *Charlotte Temple*, became a hit in England; in 1790, it came out in a U.S. edition — the nation's first bestselling novel (it went through 200-plus editions).

Despite Susanna's royalties, the Rowsons still weren't cutting it financially. This time around, both

Susanna and husband took to the stage. A natural actress, she also danced, sang, and played the guitar and the harpsichord with great verve. The couple did a tour of Scotland and England, then of the American cities of Philadelphia, Baltimore, Annapolis, and Boston. The word was boffo box-office. In 1796, they were offered a permanent gig at the Federal Street Theatre in Boston. Susanna spent more than five active years on stage.

This woman was a creative whirlwind. Besides creating drama onstage and off, she wrote seven other novels, plus poetry, songs, short stories, and several stage plays. Her most successful play, *Slaves in Algiers*, in which she starred, took a number of potshots at her era, in which both sexes conspired to believe in the notion of "dependent women".

Eventually the tireless Mrs. Rowson opened a private girls' school in Boston — using textbooks she'd written herself! Thank goodness she didn't grow the trees and make the paper, or we'd have to call her an intercontinental overachiever.

MASTERFULLY RIGHT ON

"Honey! I've just invented something else! Wanna go to London to file a patent?" echoed through the New Jersey Quaker household of SYBILLA RIGHTON MASTERS. Hubby Tom was far too busy, being an alderman and mayor and all. So forty-four-year-old Sybilla parked the four kids with him, and in 1712 made the long sea voyage to the Old World.

All the *mal-de-mer* was worth it, though, when she got her hot little hands on Patent #401, for her Indian corn (she called it "Tuscarora rice") preparation. Sybilla had devised a labor-saving way to crush corn instead of grinding it, using a series of cogwheels powered by horses or by water. Now, making cornmeal was a snap. Instead of pushing hush puppies or mush, however, Mrs. Masters decided to tout cornmeal as the cure for tuberculosis. Grievous to report, few consumption sufferers chose to consume her Indian corn, despite its classy pulverization.

"Back to the drawing board," she thought. In between moves from New Jersey to Philadelphia, Sybilla got busy on another invention. By 1716 she had it: a brand new way to weave straw and other materials into hats, chairs, baskets, and so on. This time, she got Tom to accompany her to London, where he (in her stead) was issued Patent #403 for her invention.

Sybilla didn't mind sharing — in fact, her husband was granted a monopoly on importing palmetto leaves from the West Indies for her bonnets. Perhaps Sybilla nursed a secret desire for big-city action, or maybe just a craving for some decent fish and chips.

At any rate, the couple stayed on in London for a year to market Sybilla's new brainchild, leaving their actual children in Philly, presumably with a caregiver. This time around, inventor Masters opened a retail shop and had much greater success at sell-through, there being more of a market for decent headgear and basketry than there was for TB cures, no matter how miraculous.

A WHIZ AT MONOPOLY

We only know this Chipewyan Indian by her whitey surname: MADAME LAMALLICE. But she made an impression on a lot of men, including her French trapper husband, who schlepped goods for the Hudson's Bay Company at Fort Wedderburn on Lake Athabasca. At the fort, trilingual Madame L found herself holding the key job — sole interpreter for the whites. Recognizing a sweet thing when she saw it, she laid a few demands on George Simpson, new leader of Fort Wedderburn: "Extra rations, please — and preferential treatment, or I walk!"

The whites, struggling to stay alive during the hideous winter of 1820-1821, acquiesced. By spring, however, food had run very low. Simpson sent word that all the trappers should take their families into the wilderness to fish. Not about to leave her cozy fireplace, Madame said, *"Non!"* to the snow job. Thrifty as well as demanding, she'd stockpiled some 200 dried fish, and had plenty to see *her* family through lean times.

Simpson got a kick out of that; he wasn't so pleased, however, to learn that Madame had also accumulated a Y2K-sized stash of ribbons and cloth, and was using them to carry on a brisk trade in meat, moose skins, and beaver tails. When he and other company officers attempted a showdown, La Lamallice showed her teeth,

134

threatening to turn the surrounding Native Americans against the whites.

All too soon came that fateful day in 1821 when the Hudson's Bay and Nor'Wester trading companies merged — a corporate move that brought more multilingual folks into the mix. No longer the only silver-tongued communicator at the fort, Madame Lamallice lost her lock on the position of Canada's powerful petticoat politician.

A FERTILE BRAIN FOR SCHEMING

Ingenious and generous — that was ELIZA LUCAS. It didn't hurt, either, being born into an affluent British colonel's family. Eliza got a jolly good education, from French to Shakespeare. Like other army brats, by her teens she'd lived in Europe, the Caribbean, and North America.

In 1738, when her father inherited three rice plantations in Carolina Colony, the Lucas family settled there. Shortly thereafter, Dad got called away to join England's new war with Spain. Instead of hiring a manager, he handed CEO duties over to his teenaged daughter — the shrewdest move he ever made.

Up every morning at five, Eliza wasn't content with time-honored ways. She innovated. A pioneer in silkworm culture, she impressed the heck out of distant royalty when she had her own silk woven into a fab gift for them. What an opportunity for name-dropping: "That reminds me of the time the Princess of Wales was wearing my silk gown . . ."

This self-taught botanist had a thing for living things — and we don't mean boyfriends. This free-spirited speller once wrote, "I love the vegitable world extremely." Eliza experimented with the notoriously fussy indigo plant (source of the best blue dye of the day) and got it to flourish on local soil. In 1744, this green thumb raised indigo for seed only — then gave it,

136

and her cultivation secrets, to any planter who would grow it. The colony soon shipped more than 100,000 pounds of indigo to England, winning praise for Eliza — and a tasty tax break for her and the other colonists.

Running plantations, coping with her sickly mom, and playing the flute when she had a free moment, Eliza evaded marriage for years. Daddy sent two write-in candidates, adroitly rejected by Eliza. She remained a Miss until age twenty-two, when love persuaded her to wed forty-five-year-old widower Charles Pinckney.

An eventual three-time mom, Eliza kept her fertile brain a-boil, studying law and other such frivolous pastimes. After her husband expired of malaria, new widow Pinckney became a hands-on planter again. Now with even more plantations to run, Eliza spent the next forty years zestfully carrying out her best ideas, from growing figs for export to teaching her slave girls to read and write. When Eliza Lucas Pinckney died of cancer on May 26, 1793, George Washington was among those who asked to be a pall-bearer for the woman who had honored her "own true self", as she put it.

It's pleasant to find that Eliza's traits duly survived in her only daughter, HARRIOTT HORRY, who also married late, got widowed early, stayed single, ran a plantation, and savored life to the fullest.

A KINDER, GENTLER SING SING

Think of a matron at a famous federal penitentiary like Sing Sing, and you envision a crusty old gal, or a Nurse Ratchet-type. ELIZA WOOD FARNHAM was neither. At twenty-nine, this New Yorker was already a well-known social reformer when she got called to the Big House.

As women's matron, Farnham made a number of humane changes. Until her tenure, female prisoners had been allowed to work and eat together — but only in *total silence*. Talk about cruel and unusual punishment! Not surprisingly, this policy from the governing board had led to riots. As matron, Farnham brought many humanizing touches: she allowed prisoners to have books, flowers, curtains — even dolls. She also brought in a piano and encouraged singalongs and other social events.

After serving as matron for four years, a widowed Farnham moved to California, where she started a society to help women without resources migrate west.

Even after remarriage, this altruist pushed for higher education and careers for women, and wrote several worthy books, the most widely read being *Woman and Her Era*.

CHAPTER FIVE

Swashbucklers & Gender Benders

HIGH-SEAS THELMA AND LOUISE

In the late 1600s, two girls were born in the British Isles; despite the commute they would face, they eventually became the New World's most talked-about partners in crime.

Because her English granny disliked girls, MARY READ was dressed as a boy while young — a ploy that kept the support money flowing. When Granny bit the dust, Mary's mother rented her out as a footman. "Way too tame," thought the young cross-dresser; Read signed up for duty on a more macho-sounding man-of-war.

On board, Read fell for fellow limey Jules, who took her gender outing in stride. Since they shared a passion for brews, they left the sea to open a tavern in Breda. Mary had a brief flirtation with the straight life until an outbreak of peace killed business, and Jules responded to bankruptcy by dying. Mary, who thankfully hadn't taken her male duds to Goodwill, headed for the West Indies on a merchant ship. In mid-voyage, her vessel was commandeered by noted rascal Calico Jack and his pirates.

Meanwhile, ANNE BONNEY, red-haired "Louise" from County Cork, found herself in South Carolina, where her family had hastily emigrated after a lawyer-impregnates-housemaid scandal. Brawny Bonney was a brawler who ran away early and coupled casually. Always interested in breaking more commandments, Anne auditioned for the coveted job of pirate by stealing a ship and murdering its crew. "Hired!" said Calico Jack, her new employer.

It was on the decks of Jack's ship that kindred spirits Anne and Mary met. Some folks insist they were lovers. Maybe so — but we're talking pirates here, a group notoriously lax in the "Dear diary" and love letter department.

Now superbad in tandem, Bonney and Read became infamous. Mary had a gift for navigation; Anne, for personnel management and downsizing. Both loved doing violence to furniture, ships, and other humans. To relax, now and again the sexually spirited pair would jump the bones of some hottie they happened to capture.

After three years at the top of the marine "Most Wanted" list, their ship was captured in 1720 by the British Navy — and only because the crew was intoxicated. Anne, Mary, Calico Jack, and the rest were taken in irons to Jamaica for trial. Calico soon swung from a yardarm. The women, however, "pled their bellies", a useful albeit short-term ploy used by pregnant criminals to avoid the noose.

Records are murky, but Mary Read seems to have died in prison or in childbirth. Anne Bonney, on the other hand, may have gotten away. For a time, her "Wanted for Murder and Arson" posters graced taverns throughout the New World.

Although the deeds of these two "Be all that we can be" buccaneers on the bounding main should be vile enough for anyone, they continue to be romanticized and embellished upon, even today.

DANCES WITH DILEMMAS

Being the big deal squaw-sachem of the Sakonnet Indians had its moments. As the tribe's head, AWASHONKS got to lead the troops into battle, call the council meetings, and best of all, organize the tribal dances. The big A loved to dance up a sweat around the campfire.

Awashonks and her people lived near Narragansett Bay in an area now called Rhode Island — a place that quickly became too congested with the arrival of some extremely pale and fertile folks from England.

Awashonks had a special talent for negotiation and diplomacy. That saved her bacon more than once — and that of her people, a fortunate exception among Native Americans of New England.

When things started heating up between Indians and whites in the 1670s, Awashonks made an alliance with her powerful white neighbor, Colonel Benjamin Church. Her goal? To avoid being blamed for raids and other unfriendly actions carried out by other native peoples. For his part, the Colonel saw Awashonks as a shrewd leader — and was glad to accept the protection of the Sakonnets.

But things got sticky. The Wampanoag tribe, led by Metacomet (confusingly called "King Philip" by tongue-tied whites), and his emissaries came to see Awashonks in 1675. He talked just like a candidate in a

New England primary: "Just looking for your support in the general rebellion of natives we're raising."

Awashonks was busy leading a big dance in her guests' honor, which killed some time before she had to respond to Metacomet. Call her loco, but this squaw-sachem just didn't see a favorable cost/benefit ratio for her participation.

"Thanks, but we'll sit out this war," she said in her most Camp David tone.

To get her support, Metacomet tried blackmail. "We'll burn down the houses of your white neighbors, and kill their cattle. And you know who will get blamed for it, don't you?" he threatened. But Awashonks stood firm, a veritable Switzerland among Native Americans. After several years of record bloodshed on both sides, the conflict ended. She and the Sakonnets were among the tiny handful of natives who received amnesty from the victorious — but you knew that already — colonists.

PERUVIAN MOUNTIE

Cloak and dagger? Favorite ensemble for an uppity woman of sixteenth-century Peru, whose real name has faded from history. Peruvians of those Wild West times called her "NIÑA DE LA HUECA" or "Girl with the Deep Voice". Allegedly six feet tall — making her a giant among Peruvians — more muscle than curves, La Hueca was famous for getting into brawls and could throw a mean left hook. She got ample opportunity. She lived in the mountains, during a time when Bolivia ruled Peru — sorta — and political chaos reigned. When local law enforcement put out a call for recruits, La Hueca answered.

Her new job was a beat as an *encapado*, a cop on horseback, essentially. *Encapados* wore swirling cloaks or capas, giving them that creepy Sleepy Hollow look so useful for hunting down tax evaders, highway robbers, and other dregs of Peruvian society. La Niña de la Hueca thrived on her daily dirty work of swordplay and violence. When last heard of, this early Terminator led a team of four of the meanest *encapados* around, working the Andean beat between Lima and Caluma.

SPIRIT IN THE DARK

Who says sisters-in-law can't have a lark — and do a patriotic turn at the same time? During the Revolutionary War years of fighting the British, GRACE and RACHEL MARTIN would put on male clothing, strap on a pistol or two, and hide along dark South Carolina roads. Eventually, they would hear the horses of British couriers. Guns at the ready, Grace and Rachel intercepted rider after rider, taking strategic documents, emptying pouches, and forcing the men to return the way they came. On one occasion, the fed-up couriers stopped at a nearby house and asked the matron within for a night's lodging. "We're just guys on parole — nothing important, really," they claimed. Under the sympathetic gaze of their hostess, the travelers whined about being held up by "armed men". The lady of the house — who happened to be Grace's mother — had a hard time keeping a straight face, knowing that the whiners' dispatches were already on their way to American General Greene.

SHOW ME THE WAMPUM

No wonder she was called MOLLY BRANT by the British. Her tribal name: Koanwatsi-tsiaienni. She and her brother Joseph were among the leaders of the Six Nations: the Iroquois Confederacy of Mohawk, Seneca, Cayuga, Onondaga, Oneida, and Tuscarora tribes.

At twenty-three, Molly made a turn toward masochism. She took a liking to William Johnson, who hit New York to act as Superintendent for Indian Affairs of the Northern Colonies. After his first mate died in childbirth, William linked limbs with Molly. A classic male chauvinist, Johnson pooh-poohed female smarts. He wouldn't allow leaders like her to attend the negotiations he held with male chiefs. His gender blind spot didn't let him see that his own liaison with Molly gave him higher status — and negotiating firepower — among the Native Americans.

Ignoring this major slur, Molly produced a steady stream of infants with Johnson, who passed off the whole arrangement as "companionship". Later, in his will, he did leave Molly his estate — but smarmily called her "my prudent & faithfull Housekeeper". She'd lived at lavish Johnson Hall for fifteen years. About ten minutes after the funeral, however, his eldest son from the first marriage bumped Molly from the luxury berth. With a shrug, she settled on a piece of land from her estate.

146

Kids and homemaking weren't really Brant's medicine pouch, anyway. She preferred to keep her hand in politically. With her work and wise counsel, for years she kept the Indian confederacy loyal to the Brits, who used warriors against their traditional foe, the French. As an awed admirer said, "One word from her goes farther with the Indians than a thousand from any white man."

Then that dratted Revolutionary War flared up. The Redcoats had tremendous allies in Molly and the Iroquois, who saw that grabby colonists were pushing them out of traditional territories. Egged on by the equally grabby Brits, Iroquois warriors pulled off some spectacular massacres and white hostage-taking. Uh-oh. That got the Yanks mad enough to win.

When the smoke cleared in 1783, the Brits and the Six Nations were whipped. Abandoning her lands in New York and hightailing it into Canada with the rest, Molly Brant settled in Ontario.

Molly might have been Mohawk, but she didn't go for that "we're just caretakers of the land" philosophy so dear to Indians on the silver screen. Before she'd even unpacked, she'd filed with the Loyalist Claims office in London. In time, she got a tidy compensation for the loss of her land, and an annual pension of 100 pounds, which kept her nicely until her death at age sixty.

A DIFFERENT KIND OF CABIN FEVER

Poor and Irish, POLLY MULHOLLIN got to America the old-fashioned way — by indenturing herself as a servant for seven years. Once her servitude was up, Polly caught wind of a government offer: "Free land!" it shouted. "No strings attached! Just clear a mere hundred acres of forest, throw a cabin on it, and it's yours for life!"

Amid the hyped-up verbiage, the young Irishwoman spotted a wilderness-sized loophole in the offer: Nowhere did it say that you had to live in the cabin you built in order to claim the real estate.

Glad to have flexed her mental muscles for a change, Mulhollin headed for the western frontier — at that time, the far reaches of Virginia and Kentucky — and waded in. Fortunately, seven years of laundry and firewood chopping had given her the wind and the build of a lumberjack. Dressed in vaguely male grubbies, Polly sawed away, clearing her acreage and putting up a cabin in record time.

That dwelling became "cabin rights" central for Mulhollin, who then moved through virgin forest like a giant termite, felling trees and erecting cabins — twenty-nine more of them! You might wonder: Besides build cabins, what the heck did she do with all those logs? Burned 'em. In colonial times, cabins had open fireplaces in each room, and people went through more than thirty cords of wood a year. That's an acre of forest.

Eventually Polly put on a clean pair of moccasins, went into town, and claimed her 3,000 acres on Virginia's border. What's more, she kept them. Eventually this sawdust-covered pioneer met an admiring man, married, and started producing her own family tree with as much verve as she had felled a forest. Or two.

EARLY AMERICAN PYRAMID SCHEME

Among the Blackfoot Indians of the Northwest, being called Ko-come-ne-pe-ca or "MANLIKE WOMAN" was probably a compliment. Bright and belligerent, this Blackfoot had a devil-may-care attitude about what other people, red or white, thought. In the early 1800s, she hooked up with a white fellow who worked for the Nor'Wester traders, but continued to play the field.

Eventually she was kicked out of the Blackfoot bunch, shook off her trader, and headed for greener fields with the Okanagan Indians farther up the Columbia River. Once there, Manlike breezed into camp, proclaiming that (1) she had big medicine, thanks to the magical letters she was carrying for the white traders, (2) she was a shaman, and (3) she was a man. Didn't her male attire prove it?

Impressed by her eccentric showmanship, the Okanagans bought it. Buoyed by her success, Manlike looked around for other fair game. In 1811, she chose a female companion and headed downriver to Fort Astoria, where a new settlement of white traders had just arrived. After flimflamming them with her shaman tales and her glowing recommendations as a postal worker, Manlike Woman said, "I can help you! Let's explore and exploit the interior together!"

After loading up on free samples of barter items, she and her new squeeze worked their way back upriver,

150

now spreading the word that white traders were on their way. "See this stuff? Check it out — real axes! They're bringing more — and it's all free!"

Of course there was a catch. In order to be among the lucky recipients, the Indians had to give the wily promise-maker some good-faith goodies — and a horse on which to carry them. It became a neat pyramid scheme. As each successive tribe saw the wealth piled high on Manlike's train of ponies, they felt a deep need to outdo the previous tribes.

By the time Manlike Woman reached the safety of the Okanagan tribal grounds, she had a string of twenty-six animals laden with material wealth from gullible whites and Native Americans alike. That feat was proof enough for the Okanagans of her leadership qualities: they promptly made her chief.

GAY CABALLERAS

Lucky little orphan ANNIE LEZAMA DE URINZA — in seventeenth-century Peru, she managed to find a congenial home with the de Sonza family — and in that well-heeled household, encountered a fellow mischief-maker in their daughter, EUSTAQUIA.

As good Catholic girls, Annie and Eustaquia were pushed to do needlework. Instead, they lobbied to take fencing lessons, like Eustaquia's big brother. After his early demise (curiously convenient!), the sorrowing parents gave the two girls a fencing master — and a firing range of their very own at Casa de Sonza.

In the rowdy world just outside the de Sonza door, the people of Potosí were busy attending bullfights, going to fiestas, and shooting one another in duels. Not that the girls got in on any of it; as youngsters, they had to be content with secondhand street gossip from a servant or two.

As hormones hit, however, they learned the teenage ways of sneaking out of the hacienda. From the outset, Annie and Eustaquia favored male caballero getups — a habit that got them into various street fights. One memorable night, the teenaged caballeras fought against four, whipping the cutlasses off their ruffian attackers while sustaining a number of wounds themselves. (Given the state of their clothes after these evenings, the laundress for the de Sonzas must have gotten some handsome hush money.)

152

Finally the great day arrived: Eustaquia came into her inheritance. By now the two young women were inseparable. And romantically intertwined. Rattling their sabers, clutching their autobiographies of Catalina de Erauso, a cross-dressing role model, the two set off on horseback, anxious for further adventures. The next five years wouldn't disappoint. Peru was still the Wild West of South America, and Annie and Eustaquia became part of its mystique.

Returning to Potosí, Annie decided to concentrate on *rejoneo*, the art of fighting bulls from horseback. She got very good at it. Only trouble was, the bull was better. In one painful corrida, she got gored. "Only a flesh wound!" she proclaimed. But gorings have a nasty habit of getting infected; Annie's did, and after a long illness, she died. A few months later, her bereft lover quit this Earth too.

After Eustaquia and Annie made herstory, a prolific writer named Bartolomé Arzans made hay. Turned on by a portrait of the two female warriors, whom he thought "handsome and erotic", in 1736 he wrote a history of Potosí that profiled the astonishing pair. His account, which weighed in at a million words or so, is still being used as a doorstop in remote corners of Peru.

LAME EXCUSES? WE GOT 'EM!

One of Virginia's few soldiers with two X chromosomes, ANNA MARIA LANE served with honor in the Revolutionary War. With her husband John, she fought bravely at the battle of Germantown — even got wounded and lamed for life. Think that cut any mustard with the folks handing out postwar pensions at the Virginia General Assembly? No. At least, not immediately.

But Anna Maria kept on their case. Year after year. Decade after (yawn) decade. The whole affair came to a brilliant conclusion on February 6, 1808 — a mere twenty-seven years after the war's end — when the Assembly bestirred itself to recognize Lane's "extraordinary military services." They bestowed on her an annual pension of $100 a year for life. As they told her more than once, "Hey lady! That's more than double what yer husband got." Satisfying as that moment must have been, Lane managed to collect her pension just twice before quitting the planet. For Virginia bean-counters, patriotic procrastination had paid off.

SECRET SEX IN HAVANA

By the time she'd been practicing *medicina* for ten years, a sly señorita named HENRIETTA FABER decided it was time to come clean. She'd already taken up handwashing, a newfangled notion from the doctors to the north of her home turf of Cuba. Those gringos knew a thing or two. Instead of dying like flies, her patients merely died like patients. But in 1820, "Señor" Dr. Faber also wanted to come clean about her gender. Surely by now, with her track record, she'd be accepted by the community.

Her announcement that she was still a doctor but no longer an Enrique, however, produced a Cuban *médico* crisis. Although there were cross-dressing precedents clear back to the ancient Greeks, male physicians were outraged. Black bag and all, Dr. Henrietta quickly found herself doing a mambo into the Cuban *calabozo* for ten years. The charge? "Working as a female physician".

PEACE PIPE: USE IT OR LOSE IT

Agi-ga-u-e, best known to whites as NANCY WARD, was a member of the Cherokee nation, a woman who went from "Indian" to "chief" during the Battle of Taliwa. Her husband Kingfisher caught a stray tomahawk in a vital organ, leaving his teenaged widow to take his place as war chief. So irate was she that the Cherokees easily whipped their opponents. Post-massacre, Nancy was given the high honor of being the tribe's next Ghigan, a title that could mean "Beloved Woman" or "War Woman", depending on context.

She sounds like a banshee. But through most of her years, Nancy Ward acted more like a diplomat than a fighter — a high-placed Cherokee who tried to maintain a tenuous peace with the whites. As head of the Cherokee Womens' Council, and later as a member of the Council of Chiefs, she gained even more firepower, politically speaking.

Somewhere along the way, Nancy met an amiable white trader named Brian Ward; they shared a teepee for a few years. That relationship, along with her rumored white blood from her father's side, may have given her insights into the trouble the Cherokees faced in dealing with Europeans.

Better than most, Beloved Woman saw how native peoples were inevitably going to lose ground to the flood of newcomers bent on colonizing. Committing

156

atrocities, while fun and very good for venting anger, was counterproductive. The Cherokees' only hope was to cut the best deal they could.

But Nancy's wise counsel was ignored in 1776. Facing the southern militia, the Cherokees went down to bitter defeat. In the end, they lost their traditional territories, a largely pristine area covering parts of Tennessee, North Carolina, and more than half the state of South Carolina.

WAR VET — AND AFTER-DINNER SPEAKER

DEBORAH SAMPSON's story has lots of ironies. Her Plympton family tree was heavy with big names — Miles Standish, Priscilla Alden, you name it. Three generations later, however, the Sampsons faced poverty. From age six, Deborah was "rented out" to work.

By age eighteen, well-muscled Deborah was taller than most men, a hazel-eyed woman with a deep voice who didn't say much or smile often. Handy with an axe, deft with a needle, she'd taught herself to do math, read, and write. Her literacy won her several teaching jobs. But revolution was in the air; she didn't want to darn socks, she wanted to enlist, darn it. Wearing male clothes, she signed up as "Tim Thayer", got her bonus, and hit the pub for a celebration. Uh-oh: busted! (Never drink locally, she learned.) Later, she tried again by walking to New Bedford and signing on with a ship — only to back out when she found out its captain had a Bligh-like reputation.

Finally, posing as Robert Shurtlieff, Deborah hiked seventy-five miles to the Boston area to enlist. Now in standard-issue blue coat and breeches, she marched to West Point with the Massachusetts Regiment, carrying her bayonet, firearm, and other military equipment.

It's likely that "Robert" saw action in four battles; she was wounded twice, without anyone finding her out. Instead, illness unmasked her. In 1783, ticked over being unpaid, soldiers threatened the members of Congress with violence. Ordered to Philadelphia to defend the politicos, Deborah collapsed with a high fever (Congress affects some people that way). While tending to the unconscious soldier, a Dr. Binney discovered that this was no Robert. However, the officers and men she'd served with valued her. Result: an honorable discharge.

By 1784, the press had jumped on it. The New York *Independent Gazette* ran a breathless piece about "a comely young nymph, dressed in man's apparel . . . She displayed herself with activity, alertness, chastity and valour, having been in several skirmishes . . ."

Now back in skirts, Sampson married a horse fancier named Gannett and began a family. In 1802, marching again to her own drummer, she did a lecture circuit of New York, Massachusetts, and Rhode Island. After each speech, the forty-two-year-old vet did a military drill with her rifle that brought the house down.

All very gratifying, but the bottom-line fact remained: Deborah and family were perennially poor. In 1804, Paul Revere's help got her a military pension, but even then, life was a struggle. After Deborah's death in 1827, her husband made Ripley's "Believe It or Not" by bagging the first "widower's pension" ever awarded.

This Revolutionary veteran now occupies a place of honor at the WIMSA (Women In Military Service for America) living memorial in Arlington. Besides books about her, there are streets, schools, a gladiolus, and best of all, a liberty ship named for the trailblazing New Englander who defended her country.

SHIVERING YOUR TIMBERS: NOT AS EASY AS IT LOOKS

A woman with a sharp tongue in her head, and a sharper sword in her scabbard, ANNE DIEU-LE-VEUT came from Brittany, France, drawn to the free-form Caribbean "republics" of Santo Domingo (later Haiti) and Tortuga by the prospect of a piratical future. Upon arrival, in the 1660s, she married Pierre, a local buccaneer. Only after the ceremony did she find out that Pierre was going through pirate rehab: he'd already founded a town and was planning more embarrassing good deeds, when he up and died.

Anne got very testy at being the widow of such a wuss. Other pirates disparaged her, and she took to aiming pistols at their privates. One of her targets, however, a pirate named Laurent de Graffe, begged for mercy so nicely that Dieu-le-veut decided to drag him to the altar.

Now, by God, she was gonna have a social life and a career. She went on all of Laurent's raids, and was looked upon by the crew as a regular lucky charm. Then the warranty ran out on her good fortune. In a fierce battle with a nicely laden Spanish ship, a cannonball found its mark and tore poor Laurent in two.

Everyone took time out to rubberneck. The carnage of Anne's expired husband was awesome. Pulling herself together, Anne took command of the ship and shouted in her best piratese, "Get back to the fight, me buckos!" She averted a boarding by the Spaniards, then went on the attack. In short order, the pirates' boarding hooks were digging into the sides of the galleon with a satisfying crunch.

"We've won!" Anne screeched, starting a victory conga-line; but her joy was short lived. Spanish reinforcements arrived, wounding the female buccaneer and taking most of the crew prisoner, including her.

No one quite knows what became of Anne; however, it's said, she left behind a cranky daughter who inherited her mother's testosterone-laden bluster, and went through life dueling with any fellow foolish enough to ask for her hand.

FAKE FUR-BEARER

Orkney Island off Scotland was too wee for the likes of ISABELLE GUNN, who vagabonded to the New World in 1806 to work for the Hudson's Bay Company. Since Hudson's only employed men, Isabelle did some fudging at her job interview. Posing as "John Fubister", she was duly hired. Completely alone, she canoed thousands of miles through inland waterways, moving furs and supplies wherever they were needed.

Well, maybe not always alone. Around Christmas 1807, she was partying at the Pembina trading post on the Red River. At a certain point, the faux Fubister asked her host for a place to lie down. Too much tipple? More like too much whoopee. The next day, her host wrote in his diary: "I was surprised at the fellow's demand . . . later was much surprised to find him extended on the hearth, uttering dreadful lamentations." An hour later, the host got surprise number three: a baby boy popped out onto the bear rug.

Clutching the first white child born in early Canada, Isabelle canoed to Fort Albany in the spring, working as she went. One trapper admiringly said, "She worked like anything . . . like the rest of the men." But the downside of being frankly female soon materialized; Isabelle found herself on the pearl-diving detail in the fort's kitchen, when she wasn't minding the officers' kids.

With no discrimination-suit-hungry lawyers around, Isabelle fumed but kept her mouth shut. At least she was employed. But not for long; under protest, Gunn and her illegitimate child were sent back to Orkney in the fall of 1809. Adopting the maxim, "Never explain, never apologize", Gunn unabashedly took up residence in her hometown, remaining boldly single, underemployed as a stocking knitter, and mostly impoverished until her death in 1861.

TEEN PATRIOT MOPS UP

At sixteen, MARY HOOKS SLOCUMB had already wed a troop commander in North Carolina and had a young child. But in 1776, this teen took an active though underreported role in the Battle of Moore's Creek Bridge, a sanguinary conflict that shed more type O on both sides than almost any other in the Revolutionary War.

At first, Mary was safe at home, having seen her husband and eighty others off to war. On February 27, she awoke from a vivid dream of seeing his body, and others', bloodied and dead. Alarmed, she saddled her mare, left her child with a servant, and rode forty miles to the battlefield.

At her first sight of twenty wounded men, Mrs. Slocumb dismounted and applied herbal remedies and pressure bandages to heads and bodies. With her curative skills, Mary stopped many a man from dying from blood loss on the field that day, including a friend, Frank Cogdell, who'd taken a bullet in the head and one through the thigh. At length, her own husband showed up, covered with mud and blood (most of it not his own, fortunately) and joked, "What are you doing here, Mary? Hugging Frank, the biggest reprobate in the army?"

Wisely, Mary didn't reveal her nightmare motive for coming. By now, the battle was over. The Americans

165

had won it. As she later wrote in her journal, "I was so happy — and so were all! It was a glorious victory." Late that night, she rode home alone, refusing offers to accompany her.

There had been lots of guts on display on the battlefield. But Mary Hooks Slocumb showed just as many. And throughout her seventy-six years of life, Mary insisted on wearing nothing but homespun cloth, boycotting British goods as a good patriot should.

THERE WAS SOMETHING ABOUT MARY

Weirdness had a way of dogging MARY ANNE TALBOT. Like the time she became an actress and got arrested. Not for acting — for wearing hair powder without a license. Or the night a bellicose beautician mistook her for a rival, beating Mary up badly enough to send her to the hospital.

Talbot did best when she eschewed the whole female thing and became "John Taylor". As a male, she sailed several seas, saw the New World, and served as cannon fodder in various militaries.

Her guardian, a Mr. Sucker, had fobbed off orphan Mary at age fifteen to an abusive military captain, who used her as a footboy and bed-toy en route to the West Indies. She'd barely tasted her first piña colada when it was, "Good-bye, Caribbean!" Back to Europe, where the captain signed her up as John Taylor, a drummer boy for the English Army.

In 1792, she dutifully drummed up to the front lines in Flanders, where new and exciting atrocities awaited, then into the siege of Valenciennes, France, where hundreds fell dead around her, many trampled to death by horses. Swell news: Her captain was among those trampled!

Despite two battle wounds, drummer boy now a stole a sailor's uniform, hiked to the coast, and hopped on a French vessel that was handy. Too handy, perhaps.

167

To her chagrin, Mary found she'd signed on with a privateer — a polite term for pirate.

And so it went: Talbot's gig as a powder-monkey on the British ship Brunswick went swimmingly — until she took a bullet in the thigh. She became a midshipman on another vessel, only to become a POW in a Dunkirk prison. Still, she had a dungeon mate who did the nicest gold filigree work — and Mary learned a trade she could use on land.

In 1796, she was released in a prisoner exchange. Instead of rehab, still-game Mary Anne signed on as a junior officer on an American vessel. She got a gander at New York and Rhode Island, all right, but during shore leave was hit on by an ardent young woman, necessitating her quick exit.

Talbot never did a very good job of collecting wages. On her return from the New World, and penniless again, a highwayman offered her work. Mary was totally fed up to find that the job required an entirely new wardrobe of buckskin breeches and high boots. "Why, that's highway robbery!" she squawked and opted for a job using her filigree skills.

Given her high-mileage résumé, her war wounds, and her wacky hardships, you won't be too surprised to learn that Mary Anne Talbot, a.k.a. John Taylor, departed this world in her third decade.

BRAZILIAN BRAVEHEART

Down on the farm in Bahia, Brazil, MARIA QUITEIRA DE JESÚS did a little weaving, a little spinning. But what she really enjoyed were her sessions on the shooting range with her dad. With no brothers to hog his affections, Maria got the lion's share of the attention — and of the ammo. One day around 1818, a recruiter showed up at the ranch, babbling on about how happy Brazil might be if it ever got its independence — and oh by the way, got any sons to serve as soldiers? Maria got all fired up. Not so Papa, who told the fellow, "All I've got are slaves; somehow, I don't think they'll be motivated."

Maria whined, "What about letting me go?" and got nowhere. With patriotism burning in her innards, she stole away to her older, married sister's house. Big sis, who must have had a flair for cross-dressing, outfitted Maria as a young man. Soon Quiteira was busting her buns in the army for independence. She must have been good, too. In 1823, she even got decorated for heroism by the new leader of Brazil.

As part of the deal, she got her portrait painted in uniform — holding her musket, her medal gleaming on her jacket, and wearing one of those goofy cockaded hats they favored in the nineteenth century. But Maria Quiteira de Jesús had given a new twist to the dress code: from the waist down, she'd draped herself in a Scottish kilt.

169

CHAPTER
SIX

Game Dames &
Granite Grannies

THE CALORIES FOR CONVENTS CAMPAIGN

They may have been barefoot Carmelites in seventeenth-century Mexico City, but Sisters INÉS DE LA CRUZ and MARIANA DE LA ENCARNACIÓN were far from austere. At least, that's what a gluttonous friar named García thought. Almost every afternoon, he dropped by the convent of Jesus and Mary to scarf up the eats and enjoy the organ music and the tunes belted out by this nunly duo. A connoisseur of ballads, booze, and baked goods, García was in heaven. The cookies! The two-part harmony! That divine hot chocolate the sisters made!

Plying the good friar with goodies gastronomic and musical was all part of the funding game pursued by Inés and Mariana, who sought serious pesos to build a new, austere-for-real convent. García had a good chance of making the post of viceroy. Therefore, following the eleventh commandment, "Thou shalt best reach a cleric's funds through his gut", the nuns piled on the pastry. Between gulps and slurps, the friar eventually promised to set aside building funds. When García made the top job in 1611, however, he slyly siphoned off the pork-barrel monies into a special private ring for bullfighting, which he adored even more than Inés's chocolate or Mariana's melodies. The sisters were incensed. Holy hot chocolate — García even scheduled a bullfight on Good Friday! Inés ripped off a reprimand, warning García, "*Diós* is gonna getcha!"

Right on schedule, the nuns got an answer to their 911 prayer line. A quake postponed the first bullfight. During the second *fiesta brava*, a violent tremor threw down houses, grandstands, and walls. *Torero* fan García almost caught a boulder on the head.

"Oh well, close doesn't count," the new viceroy told himself. But that disaster was just the start. During his term of office, a dead acrobat nearly bashed the archbishop; seismic rumblings continued, followed by ash showers, floods, and a solar eclipse. To top it all off, García got sick.

Now he begged the sisters to put in a good word with *El Gran Poder*, and he'd fund their nunnery for real — but they weren't biting. Seeing by his face he was a goner anyway, Inés said, "Get ready to say *adiós* to this world." Then she marched out the door, grant applications in hand. Four years after García gobbled his last tea biscuit, these Carmelite cofounders had their new convent — and they didn't have to bake a single tart or warble a chorus of "La Cucaracha" to get it.

A TRULY TERRIFYING ROLE MODEL

Being a six-foot Georgian would have made NANCY HART stand out in almost any crowd. Add ketchup-red hair, crossed eyes, and an irascible temper to the picture, and you've got a formidable woman. Or opponent, as was more often the case.

Mrs. Hart had a husband, Ben, in the picture somewhere, and a clutch of eight children or so. The Harts lived in a cabin along the Broad River in Georgia. Early in the revolutionary conflict, stories began circulating about Nancy's scary exploits. It was said that she'd thrown a vat of red-hot lye into the face of an enemy agent. On another occasion, she'd dressed in male clothing, bullied her way into a British fort, then pretended to be a "harmless madman" so she could learn about their upcoming battle plans.

But the act she became most famous for involved six Tory soldiers who had the misfortune to pick Mrs. Hart's place as a target. (Her squeamish husband, along with other terrified neighbors, may have already fled into the swamps.) The Brits had just finished killing a soldier or two and, naturally, they were hungry. They marched into her house, commandeering the dinner that Nancy was preparing.

Eat up, drink your fill, she invited — meanwhile lifting their rifles and sending one of her eight kids to bring reinforcements. Not that Nancy needed much help; according to which account you believe, she plugged at least a couple of her unwelcome guests and held the rest of the tipsy and terrified soldiers at gunpoint. When help arrived, they all had a jolly postprandial insta-trial and hanging in Nancy's front yard.

Hart's name kept its heroically murderous fame long after she died in the 1830s. In fact, the women of LaGrange, Georgia, began their own female militia during the Civil War, and called themselves the Nancy Harts. Today you'll find even more echoes of her in northeast Georgia, from the Nancy Hart Highway to a replica of her log cabin in Nancy Hart State Park.

THE BIG EASY'S BULLET-PROOF BUILDER

Few think of New Orleans as a city of Spanish influence. French, Cajun, African-American, yes. But Hispanic? Nevertheless, two of the Big Easy's greatest benefactors, during a time when the city needed it most, were father and daughter Spanish philanthropists. Her name: MICAELA ALMONASTER, Baroness of Pontalba; his was Andrés Almonaster y Rojas.

In 1769, shipping merchant Andrés found himself in New Orleans, now a Spanish possession. Frankly, the port was a pit — mud streets, crummy buildings, zero charm. (Cheap, however — after ten years of buying bargain properties, Almonaster became rich.) At this point, Almonaster decided he'd foot the bill to give the city a new look. Who knew there'd be such a string of disasters? Fires. Hurricanes. More fires. An old man of seventy by 1795, when his daughter Micaela was born, Andrés had lost count of the structures he'd built and rebuilt: hospitals, convents, civic buildings, the cathedral, the customs house . . .

When she grew up, Micaela added to her father's legacy. But first, the spunky redhead had to survive her marriage — and her inlaws. Wed at fifteen to a French baron, she was living in the family chateau near Paris when her father-in-law went ballistic one night and shot her four times in the chest before pumping a bullet into his own bent brain.

174

No fortune is worth this hassle, declared Micaela, and gingerly traveled back to New Orleans with her three sons. There, dressed in jodhpurs so she'd be taken seriously, the now-fit baroness personally oversaw the design and construction of two buildings she named the Pontalbas. On family property located on two sides of Jackson Square, she built a series of graceful three-story apartments, with shops on the ground floor. They still border the square, the heart of old New Orleans and today's city as well. No shrinking violet when it came to taking credit, Micaela put her family's initials — "A" for Almonaster, "P" for Pontalba — on the decorative iron balconies, where you can still admire them today.

BUBBLE TROUBLE

When she could barely see over a washtub, ELLEANOR ELDRIDGE began work for the Baker family in Warwick, Rhode Island, washing clothes for 25 cents. That's per week, not per garment. Those tedious hours bent over a scrub board weren't wasted — they merely motivated Elleanor to get into weaving, spinning, and making her own soap.

By her twenties, she and her sister ran a business in those services. Despite her modest income, Elleanor knew how to save. As soon as she'd amassed enough, she bought a lot, built a house, and rented it out for $40 a year. Another ten years or so, and Miss Eldridge had a nest egg for a bigger house. What with her add-ons, house rentals, and various enterprises, by the early 1800s this nonstop black entrepreneur had doggedly built herself a net worth of more than $4,000 in property alone.

But into each life, however blameless, some precipitation must fall. Miss Eldridge finally took a vacation to visit kinfolk. The words *Eldridge* and *time off* had never been linked before; perhaps that's why the rumor began that Miss Elleanor had died.

The happy vacationer came back to find her property sold. Now she had to go to court, where she filed a trespass-and-eject suit. But you know the legal system. Sometimes even when you win, you lose. Miss Eldridge got the catch-22 news: You've won your case! Once you fork over $2,700, you can recover your property!

Despite this slippery reversal of fortune, the Queen of Suds kept on making bubbles — and money. This Rhode Island legend became an inspiration to many, affectionately remembered by her community, and written about in a history by Frances Whipple.

BE ALL THAT CARABOO CAN BE

Abused teen. Poor family from Devon, England. No wonder MARY WILLCOCKS ran away and joined a band of gypsies. Travel! Exotic costumes! Jail time! Her gypsy band only got as far as London, but Mary picked up priceless on-the-con skills — from tambourine banging to high-quality begging. Before long, she also picked up a husband, a vagabond with a smattering of exotic languages — which she also absorbed before he took a powder and disappeared.

Around 1815, Mary reinvented herself as "Princess Caraboo". Dressed in a feathered headdress and vaguely Far Eastern garments, armed with bow and arrow, speaking in pantomime and a tongue from her "own" distant country, Mary knocked on doors until Pastor Worrall and his wife took her — and her story — in. As Mary described, she'd been kidnapped and sold to a ship captain headed for Europe, and had just escaped his clutches. Her unusual antics — sleeping on the floor, perching in trees, jumping in the lake fully clothed — kept the fiction alive.

The ersatz princess milked the Worralls for all they were worth, then went from Gloucestershire to Bath, where she bathed in a new round of celebrity. The papers played up the princess magnificently. She got lots of awed attention. Maybe too much; a sharp landlady in Bristol saw her tale and said, "That's no

178

princess — that's my old lodger, Mary Baker!" Even after the revelation, kind-hearted Mrs. Worrall was sure the whole thing was a media mix-up. Unmasked at last, Caraboo unburdened herself. Her authentic tale of tragedy and adventure won over Mrs. W even more.

"What can I do to help this poor girl?" Mrs. Worrall wondered. "How about a ticket to the United States?" Caraboo responded. Mrs. Worrall soon had her packed, paid for, and on a ship — with a party of missionaries to look after her.

New-World bound, Caraboo Mary found her kindly-meant chaperones a bit restrictive. As the ship moved through the Atlantic, she learned they were nearing St. Helena, the tiny island where Napoleon Bonaparte sulked in exile. In a flash, Mary made an executive decision, stole a lifeboat, and rowed ashore — there to enchant at least some of Bonaparte's remaining evenings as his exotic companion.

Persistent rumor had it that Princess Caraboo spent the last part of her life in London, selling leeches — the perfect commodity for a woman who'd done more than a little fiscal liposuction herself.

QUAKER IRONY

Brandywine Iron Works co-owner REBECCA PENNOCK LUKENS had her hands full with three kids and a newborn baby, when in 1825 her loving husband did the meanest thing: he died. Besides draping crepe, her mill-hands wanted to know: What about the huge order the plant had received to make plate for the USS *Codorus*, the first American ironclad warship?

Full speed ahead, said Rebecca. But first she had to battle her cranky mother, her crankier bank, her husband's lack of a will, her dad's ambiguous will, and her own learning curve. Behind schedule, the company was also teetering near bankruptcy from expansion. With her brother-in-law overseeing the plant, Lukens tackled arcane matters, from squeezing out financing to purchasing raw materials. Solo, she learned to deliver orders on time — and set prices that turned a profit. After a near-speed-of-light effort, the *Codorus* order was duly delivered to York, Pennsylvania.

From that stressful beginning, Rebecca built her company into a major player in the iron plate biz. Besides commissions for seagoing vessels, she won contracts to make locomotives and Mississippi steamboats. With her at the helm, her company weathered the financial panic of 1837.

Through it all, her Quaker mom had the same refrain: "Thou art out of line!" Not easy to ignore the old bat either, since she carried the debt on Rebecca's enterprise. Lukens had other opposition — some of it even from outside her family. The mills downstream, for instance, whose owners leaned on her for more water. Rebecca just leaned back.

Being Quakers, her Pennsylvania family held the philosophy that women had brains and potential. As a student, Rebecca had waded into higher math, French, botany, chemistry, and "static electricity" (not a major you see much any more). She'd tagged after her dad in the mill, seeing how sheets or iron were slitted into rods for blacksmith use. After her marriage, she got further industry insights. She'd come to agree with her husband that big iron plates — and big contracts — represented their future.

Over time, Rebecca Lukens became a woman of wealth, a leading citizen, and an enlightened employer. She built houses for her workers, awarded bonuses for reaching mill output goals, and provided working conditions that were better than most of her era. Five years after her death at fifty-eight, the company honored Rebecca by renaming itself Lukens Iron Works (later, Lukens Steel Company), which it remains to this day.

GIMME DANGER — AND A DRAM

Although her nicknames, "Mad Ann" and "white squaw of the Kanawha", wouldn't pass for compliments today, Welshwoman-turned-frontiers-woman ANN BAILEY won them for her reckless ways and her sheer fearlessness, helping the U.S. Army ward off hostile Indian attacks.

She'd come to America as a poor emigrant, married, and moved to the Appalachian country of West Virginia, in the region of the Kanawha River, where her husband died in 1774. Adventurous Ann chose to stay on alone and work as a scout and messenger, even though local tribes made the area highly perilous for white settlers.

Native Americans were a little weirded out by this maniacally hardy individualist. After all, the way she forded rivers, built rafts, and tracked her way through complete wilderness was supposed to be *their* shtick. Clad in buckskins, Bailey was hardly ever harassed by Indians — except verbally, of course.

In 1791, Ann's trek to Fort Lee won widespread admiration. Armed with a pocket compass, a rifle, an axe, and a flask of spirits, the short, stoutly built horsewoman made a 200-mile solo ride to bring ammunition to the besieged fort. On her way to and from this and other rescues, she recruited men to fight in the Indian wars and did a bit of spying as well.

182

In 1826, near the end of her life, Bailey was interviewed by journalist ANNE ROYALL for her book, *Sketches of History, Life, and Manners in the United States*. An early Barbara Walters, Royall asked Bailey, "What would the General say to you, when you finally got safely to camp with your ammunition?" Ann answered, "Why, he'd say, 'You're a brave soldier, Ann,' and tell some of the men to pour me a dram of whiskey."

Journalist Royall, whose own liquor bill was probably substantial for these interviews, added, "She was fond of a dram . . . I shall never forget Ann Bailey."

And we shouldn't, either.

YOU GIVE ME FEVER

ANNA BELKNAP and other hardworking female pioneers were just getting the hang of homesteading in 1848 when gold fever hit Oregon's Willamette Valley. Like a shot, most males and more than a few fit females headed for them thar hills of California, leaving Oregon bereft of upper-body strength. Mrs. Belknap, whose land claim and family of young 'uns kept her hopping, wrote a journal about those times.

As she remarked, "If it had not been for our Indian neighbors, not many of us could have survived. We traded with them for smoked salmon and fresh venison — and they could be counted on to do whatever they were paid for, cutting firewood or farming duties. Except milking a cow. To the Indians, that was a disgrace."

At length, gold-seekers of both sexes straggled back to the Northwest, most with nothing to show for it except bad nails and a good tan. Some nugget-maddened souls never returned — killed over claims, or still gambling on making a strike. As Belknap wrote, "Gold broke up more homes in that day and age than alcohol ever did."

BACK TO HER ROOTS

As the daughter of the governor of South Carolina, MARTHA LOGAN didn't need to bother her pretty li'l head about such unladylike pursuits as work. But she said "Pshaw!" to Pa, and set about becoming a school-teacher, a nursery owner, and a horticulturist of some note.

Her nursery was a shrewd marketing idea. In the mid-1700s, gardening was all the rage among the affluent on the Atlantic seaboard. Men and women of means had huge grounds around their houses, which they vied to landscape with rare specimens. At her place in Charleston, Logan grew her own flower seed, bedding plants, and shrubs. She imported more exotic varieties from London, selling them through her nursery. When not digging in the dirt, Martha carried on a brisk twenty-year correspondence with leading botanists in the United States. She also wrote and published her *Gardener's Kalendar*, an almanac that won rave reviews.

Satisfying as the horticultural life was, it hardly sufficed for Martha, who boarded children and taught them in her home, besides managing her plantation. In her seventies, still spry and interested in living things, Martha Logan wrote a book on gardening — which won praise from *South Carolina* magazine.

COLD, COLD FORT

In 1713, a young Chipewyan Indian named THANADELTHUR was taken prisoner by the Cree Indians. After a year, she escaped, wandering for months in a hell of Canadian ice and snow, living on game from her snares. She hoped to rejoin her people. Or second best, to find traces of the white traders whose totally amazing artifacts and goods she'd seen in the Cree camp.

One spring morning, the half-starved woman tracked white hunters to York, the Hudson's Bay fort in eastern Canada. Soon Governor James Knight heard the harrowing story of "the Slave Woman", as he called her. After meeting Thanadelthur, Knight saw that her obvious intelligence, linguistic abilities, and grasp of diplomacy might help him end the war between tribes — and win some brownie points for the fur-hungry British in the process.

In 1716, they mounted an expedition of shuttle diplomacy. Thanadelthur had her hands full, placating her own people, trying to keep everyone from taking revenge on the Cree. At the same time, she was schmoozing nonstop to keep those Cree whiners from making a preemptive strike. She finally got delegations from the two enemy camps to meet. As an admiring whitey said, "She made them all stand in fear of her — she scolded at some and pushed others — forcing them to ye Peace."

186

Ye Peace mission accomplished, Thanadelthur relaxed for the winter in the York fort. During the long cold nights, Thanadelthur told tales of faraway riches to the guv, who grew eager to grab the "yellow mettle" supposedly possessed by distant Indians. Gold aside, Knight was terribly impressed with her quick mind. The two actually became friends — although he never could get the hang of her given name.

But wouldn't you know it, the Brits had skimped on the central heating (don't they still?). York fort was no match for that winter. In January, Knight wrote in his journal that "ye Northern Slave Woman has been dangerously Ill . . ." He pitched in to help nurse her — but to no avail. On February 5, 1717, Thanadelthur died. Knight wrote, "She had a very high spirit . . . the firmest resolution . . . and great courage." He finished his journal by saying, "Wee have had the finest weather any day this season but the most melancholyist by the loss of her."

IF YOU AXE ME . . .

Getting kidnapped by Indians made HANNAH DUSTON testy. For that matter, so did being a new mom. For the twelfth time. Who could blame her for taking decisive action? On March 15, 1697, she, her nurse MARY NEFF, and thirty-nine other whites had been dragged out of Haverhill, Massachusetts, and goose-stepped 100 miles into the wilderness.

Kidnap by Indians was getting to be a common occurrence in New England, especially during the protracted wars between the French, English, and native forces. But Hannah simply refused to accept this outrage.

After they arrived at an Indian village in New Hampshire, she and Mary were made servants of a family of twelve. Meanwhile, Hannah sized up the talent. Besides Mary, there was Samuel, another young prisoner held by the family, who looked sharp.

Using their best cozening skills, Hannah and Sam got a few naive natives to demonstrate the use of the tomahawk. Finally, after learning where the weaponry was kept at night, Hannah and friends awoke before dawn on March 30 and fielded their own massacre. Mrs. Duston herself whacked out nine Indians. To prove their story, Hannah worked through her anger at the whole sordid chain of events by scalping her captors!

188

Dripping — not just with sweat — and running, the three got clean away. Eventually, Hannah, Mary, and Samuel made it to Boston, where the community went bananas over their feats. Preacher Cotton Mather ate it up. He eloquently compared Hannah's courage and her spectacular sanguinary serrations to that of the Biblical Jael, who slew Sisera.

Only a couple of minor details made the comparison less than apt: Hannah had scalped six Indian *children*, along with three adults. Furthermore, she'd brought back the scalps not so much for "proof" as for the bounty.

Sure enough, the General Court in Boston paid her the princely sum of 25 pounds for her terrible trophies. Another 25 pounds went to Mary and Samuel to split. After her spectacular "woman bites dog" feat, Hannah returned to her husband and seven living kids, and led a more normal life — at least, that we *know* of.

Physical aggression may have been all in the family. No one brought it up at the time, but Hannah's sister ELIZABETH EMERSON had been executed in 1693 for killing her twin babies at birth.

FAUX SISTER, REAL DIAMONDS

She mighta been born in the sticks but she had couth; in fact, SARAH WILSON bumped stiff competition to become a servant in Queen Charlotte's court. She stuck with the job long enough to win confidence — then eloped in 1771 with a diamond necklace, a painted miniature of her favorite royal, and the queen's cutest gown.

Drat! Caught before she had a chance to fence the goods and sentenced to death, matters looked fairly gloomy for Sarah. However, at the last minute, she was told, "Cor-blimey — the queen commuted yer sentence. However — you're to be sent as a convict to . . . the American colonies."

After a woebegone Wilson accepted her ghastly fate and wobbled off the ship on the far shore, she became part of a special "Today only!" sale on English convicts. A bit of luck: her new owner appeared to be a softy. Once she was out of those unattractive hobbles, Sarah Wilson ran away, undetected.

All this time, she'd concealed her loot. Now, after a good dry cleaning, the gown looked sharp enough for her to stroll into North Carolina, introducing herself as the Marchionesse de Waldegrave — "sister of the Queen, you know". The clincher was the miniature, which Sarah wore around her neck.

Southern hospitality — it was brilliant. Being terrific snobs, the gentry vied with each other to show "the

Marchionesse" a good time. For eighteen months, Sarah floated through Carolina society, attending balls and levees, sucking up fine viands at glorious mansions, and giving extra glitter to occasions. From time to time, she gave little talks about "royal life" — for stiff fees, payable in advance.

Wilson made additional monies through influence peddling, pertly promising, "You'd be fabulous in a government post! Let me see what I can do . . ." As fast as she met governors and bigwigs, she had more names to drop. "Looking for an army commission? Let me have a word with the guv . . ."

Eventually, the real scoop from England (and disappointed influence seekers) percolated through Southern society. Sarah Wilson found her invitations dropping off. Time to vanish — and she did, leaving a coterie of puzzled groupies. When last heard from, the faux royal was headed straight for unsuspecting snobs in the Northern colonies.

HIGH-MILEAGE METHODIST

An orphan for years, and later saddled with your standard wicked stepmother, ELIZA RUGGLES of Nova Scotia had no Norman Rockwell childhood. To top it off, when she signed on in the 1830s as the wife of a churchmouse-poor Methodist clergyman, she was hit with an avalanche of familial disapproval. "You're outta the will!" she was told. Humanitarian Eliza had higher aims; with her husband, she established a school for black children, first in Canada, later in the United States. At length, the peripatetic Ruggleses took their mission all the way to Africa. Given the hideous conditions of their odyssey (all they could afford was the dreaded "missionary class"), the family members began to drop like flies. One by one, Eliza lost her three kids and mate to disease. Sadly bruised by life but still a sucker for adventure and hardship, Eliza slowly made her way back to Nova Scotia, married a farmer, and gallantly raised a new crop of kids and grandkids, whom she enchanted with her stories of African missionary life.

I WANNA DIE A DEMOCRAT

Bet the Democratic Party wishes it still had true believers like "Grandma" MARY RAMSEY WOOD. Born in Tennessee in 1787, she attended a cotillion or two as a girl, rubbed elbows with the likes of General George Washington and Thomas Jefferson, then married a Georgia man at seventeen. She was widowed in her fifties, but that didn't stop Mary from migrating west. In 1849, she stuffed her four children into a covered wagon and headed to Oregon, riding her mare, Martha Washington Pioneer. At sixty-seven, she tried marriage again, to a short-lived hotel-builder in Hillsboro. Decades passed; "Grandma" Wood hit the century mark. When folks asked about the high point of her life, she said, "When President Andy Jackson asked me to dance." A lively stepper herself, Grandma Wood lived a reputed 120 years. Before she went, she told her kin, "Don't put my body in no hearse — I've lived as a Democrat and I want to go out in a Democratic wagon." As she wished, Mary Ramsey Wood made the trip to the boneyard in a modest hack, her coffin covered with a quilt she'd carefully selected for eternity.

BONFIRE FOR ONE

Now here's a twist — a Jewish woman practicing her religion in the mid-1500s who *didn't* get persecuted! ISABEL DE AGUILAR was a New World citizen, born in Mexico (called "New Spain" back then). The beauteous daughter of a one-eyed tailor, Isabel's chances of counting a fat dowry among her assets were slim to none.

Then along came a suitor who had it all: land, great career, looks, a bright future . . . and he was Jewish! (OK, I lied about the looks and the future.) Hernando Alonso came from a Spanish village near Huelva. Pushing sixty, he was a blacksmith by trade. Alonso had gotten to the New World by joining the forces of conquistador Hernán Cortés. As a thank-you for his slaughtering services, Alonso had been given a healthy chunk of land in Actopan, in the boondocks north of Tenochtitlán (today's Mexico City).

Despite the dismaying lack of an infrastructure or even a neighborhood to live in, Isabel and Hernando were wed around 1525. They married in the Catholic Church, as *conversos* or "New Christians". Like the mother country, New Spain had a "No Jews welcome" policy. At home, the newlyweds may have kept kosher; what they certainly kept was mum.

Life was uneventful until Hernando decided to honor one of those pesky regulations for Jewish ritual

194

cleanliness. He got heavy with Isabel, forbidding her to go to Mass during her menstrual period. How this rather private information got around, *quién sabe*. Maybe Isabel griped to a talkative friend. At that time, there were Special Inquisition Agents everywhere, checking to see who really ate pork, who just pushed it around on the plate, and so forth.

Before long, a steely-eyed inquisitor or two showed up at the Alonso door with a summons for "secret Jewish practices". And who'd they haul away? The blacksmith. In 1528, to Isabel's horror and sorrow, she made an early edition of the *Guinness Book of World Records*: widow of the first Jew to be burned at the stake in the brand-new country of Mexico.

The Inquisition had a grisly way of reminding everyone of their deeds. For years to come, Isabel got to gaze at the *sanbenito* or penitential garb worn by her late husband. After his bonfire, it was nailed to the wall of her local cathedral.

SNUFF SAID

Maidservant SARAH STUART had a heady responsibility. As her mistress, old MARGARET THOMPSON, repeatedly said, her job extended beyond the grave. Even in an era of insanely high tobacco consumption, Mrs. Thompson was extreme. The woman ate, drank, and dreamed snuff, the handy-dandy whiff-it-up-your-nose candy, popular on both sides of the Atlantic Ocean.

Before she went to that big snuff-box in the sky, Mrs. T had arranged for Sarah carry out her funeral instructions. In the Old World and the New, it was traditional to place a dish of snuff inside the coffin. As each mourner paid her respects, she took a pinch. Mrs. Thompson, however, had more memorable nicotine fantasies in mind.

At the funeral dutifully organized by Sarah, Mrs. T's coffin was carried by six of the major snuff-sniffers in the parish, each wearing a beaver hat of the appropriate shade. Six old ladies followed, clutching boxes of snuff. The priest performing the funeral had his own stash. The body itself was packed in Scotch snuff. "Nothing as fragrant and refreshing as that precious powder," as Mrs. T. often said.

At the wake, Sarah Stuart distributed farewell gifts from the ardent user — special packets to friends and neighbors. Then she circulated among the guests with a

196

two-bushel "dip it yourself" basket. At the end of the day's aromatic events, most of Margaret Thompson's survivors dizzily agreed: She'd won it by a nose.

JURY PAMPERING

Simon-pure, she wasn't. But who could believe that captivating BECKY COTTON was an axe murderer? Becky's third husband had been found at the bottom of a pond with any number of notches in him. And talk about coincidence: next to him, searchers found Mrs. Cotton's two earlier mates! Sorting through the evidence, gagging investigators found a needle through the heart of Mr. Exhibit A — and traces of poison in the third body.

In 1806, Becky went on trial in Edgefield, South Carolina. The case for the prosecution was solid until the self-made widow got up to testify. Among Becky's more wholesome assets were blue eyes, active lachrymal glands, and a line of sweet-talk that would charm birds out of trees.

In short order, jurors and judge were hot to dismiss. Or just hot. Eyewitness Mason Locke Weems wrote an account of their unseemly behavior.

Despite the bodies, the jury aquitted Becky. Furthermore, some of 'em attended her next nuptials — since the groom happened to be the most pro-Becky juror on the panel! Wedding bells didn't save our Southern belle from an ultimately nasty fate, however. Victim of a tackily copycat gesture, Becky Cotton was cut down by her own murderous brother.

101 THINGS TO DO WITH A DEAD HORSE

Any Native American looking for travel and tribulations married a French trapper. Around 1795, that's what MARIE DORION, a full-blooded Sioux, did. Eventually the couple got hired as interpreters for the Missouri-to-Oregon expedition of fur-hungry John Jacob Astor.

This wasn't one of your luckier expeditions. They left Missouri in the spring. By December the starving group had barely reached eastern Oregon. Besides wading through waist-deep snow and caring for her two kids, Marie had to make a quick pit-stop on December 31, 1811, to birth her third child. The infant died, but Marie and family made it to Fort Astoria on the coast. Home at last, thought the long-suffering mom: dank, rank, flea-filled home.

Not for long. Soon husband Pierre left to trap furs, dragging Marie and kids with him. In a rerun of the Astor disaster, the Dorions were attacked in 1814 by Malheur Indians, who thoughtfully killed only Pierre. Two kids and two horses in tow, Marie intrepidly found a hiding place in the Blue Mountains. The Dorions were snowed in for fifty-three days. Luckily, Marie carried a copy of *101 Things to Do with Ye Horsemeat*. Huddled under a horsehide tent the trio munched through her equine offerings until March, when she snowshoed out to find some Walla Walla Indians with more on the menu than old Dobbin.

SLAVISH DEVOTION

Calling all moms: Sometimes feel like a slave to your teenage daughter? Things could be worse. Wait till you hear about sixteenth-century Brazil, and the for-instance of PAULA LEME, the illegitimate slave child of a rich sugar planter named Aleixo. Dad wanted to leave his daughter something — but nothing as sordid as mere money. Therefore, Paula woke up one morning to find that (1) Daddy had died, (2) she was now free, and (3) she had inherited her own mother! (Aleixo's will thoughtfully left Paula two more slaves to help Mom in bondage.) Racially and socially, things were still sorting themselves out in Brazil — which led to incongruous situations like that of the Lemes. We don't know how this literal "mother at my beck and call" worked for Paula. What we do know is that poor Mom had another alarming possibility to look forward to: if Paula died, Mom would become the slave of her other illegitimate children by Aleixo. Kinda puts that soccer mom car pool duty in perspective, doesn't it?

GAME DAMES & GRANITE GRANNIES

TOWN FOUNDER CONFOUNDS FATHER

England's ELIZABETH HADDON still had teenage acne when her Quaker family got a famous house guest: Pennsylvania Colony founder William Penn. She loved his stories of wild Indians and wide-open country. Using her already formidable talents at wheedling, young Liz talked her wealthy dad into making a stake in the New World.

"Yahoo! We're going to someplace called New Jersey!" she told the neighbors. The ink was barely dry on the sales receipt when her dad got cold feet. "Elizabeth, we're not going," he announced. "I've got some major blacksmithing contracts. Ship anchors to make! Manly stuff to do!"

Dad had lost his nerve. No prob. To the Haddons' dismay, Elizabeth insisted on going anyway. Aghast, the family hired an older housekeeper to accompany her as a "chaperone".

In 1700, twenty-year-old Miss Haddon landed on the exotic New Jersey shores and went about making a home out of her new house, set in 500 acres of forest three miles from anyone. Whew. The yard work alone was a killer. In a couple of years, Elizabeth found a solution. She popped two questions — "Do you do lawns?" and "Want to get hitched?" — to a Quaker preacher named John Estaugh, and wed him as soon as he burbled the correct answers.

The couple logged forty years together before John died. During that time, Elizabeth founded the town of Haddonfield, crossed the Atlantic three times to visit her elderly parents, and ran the local Quaker church. But she still had time to work on her marriage. John once wrote, "I'll venture to say, few, if any, in a married state, ever lived in sweeter harmony than we did." Hearty until a great age, Elizabeth kept busy as a widow for another two decades, prompting the Haddonfieldites to say glowing things about her abilities and benevolence. Elizabeth, it's clear, just plain relished every day of her life. A testimonial after her death gave more proof: "Her heart and house were open to her friends, whom to entertain seemed one of her greatest pleasures."

A century after her death, her memory was still green. In 1863, Henry Wadsworth Longfellow honored her as his heroine in his narrative poem, *Tales of a Wayside Inn*.

NICE NATIVES FINISH LAST

"White people — what a pain," thought WETAMO, a heavy hitter of the Wampanoag tribe. Her father-in-law kept one stinking band of Puritans alive through the winter of 1621, and then they spread like crabgrass. From a leadership clan herself, Wetamo wed Wamsutta, the son of a major chief. After the honeymoon, the two Ws settled in Pokanoket, the main village of the Wampanoags, to run things.

By 1662, however, the peace between natives and newcomers was sadly frayed. The whites kept naming and claiming stuff. "Oh, you're squatting on our new colony of Rhode Island," they would say, pointing to Wetamo's village and anything else that wasn't nailed down.

Then came the day when whites dragged her husband away for "interrogation", and he ended up dead. At that point, Wetamo became chief sachem, or leader, with 300 warriors at her disposal. For a whole decade, she kept her temper, and the peace, while her brother-in-law Metacomet (whom the native language-phobic Puritans called "King Philip") tried to make sense of whitey demands.

To no avail. Finally, in 1675, Wetamo and Metacomet joined forces in a resistance movement called "King Philip's War". Talk about a traumatic conflict: Wetamo went through two more husbands during this period. She also had to deal with white POWs, like the contentious MARY ROWLANDSON. Unused to being bossed by either Indians or women, Mary made a terrible captive — and after eighty-three days was cashed in for twenty pounds of goods. The Indians even threw in some tobacco, as a "We'll pay you wampum to take her" gesture.

Relieved to unload the Rowlandson problem, Wetamo went into battle, easily wiping out Lancaster, Massachusetts, and other areas. All told, the Indians destroyed twenty towns in New England and killed about 600 colonists. Nevertheless, the game went to the whites. By the summer of 1676, more than 5,000 Indians had been killed or taken to the West Indies as slaves.

Wetamo may have died by drowning; postmortem, though, worse things may have happened. One account of the period says that Native American prisoners saw her head displayed on a pole, and "made a horrible and diabolical lamentation, crying out that it was their Queen". A sorry end indeed to a proud and intelligent woman, who'd pursued peaceful coexistence until no options were left.

"LILY OF THE MOHAWKS"

The daughter of a Mohawk chieftain and an Algonquin mother who was Christian but didn't let it get around, TEKAKWITHA (her name meant "putting things in order") was born in 1656 in upstate New York. At that time, the gifts that the English, French, and Spanish had brought to the New World were still providing unpleasant surprises. Epidemics of measles and smallpox burned like forest fires through the tribes, carrying off Tekakwitha's parents.

The four-year-old didn't make out well, either. Smallpox left her with rotten hearing, poor eyesight, weak legs, and a heavily pockmarked face.

As she grew up, French Jesuits came to her village to preach. Much taken with the Catholic faith, at nineteen she converted, taking the name Kateri or Catherine. Even as a child, Tekakwitha hadn't been big on marriage. Now she was adamantly against it. The other Indians were scornful; first the ugly little orphan wants to stay single, and now she's adopted the white man's religion! Kateri got abuse from almost everyone.

Finally she fled her native village to live with other Christians at the Mission of St. Francis Xavier near Montreal. Despite her shaky health, Kateri Tekakwitha made it her mission to live a blameless holy life and to help the less fortunate. She rose at 4a.m. to go to early Mass, choosing to walk there barefoot through the

205

snow. Only after that did she get to work, ministering to the sick and aged, and teaching local children.

She inspired many other Native American masochists to make austerity and self-chastisement a life goal — from putting glowing coals between their toes to taking icy river dips in winter.

By degrees, word spread of her spirituality and her good works. Native Americans and whites alike began calling her "Lily of the Mohawks". She was barely twenty-four when she died, and a cult soon formed around her name; fellow penitents began to pray at her grave.

By 1939, Kateri Tekakwitha reached step 1 toward Catholic sainthood by being declared "venerable". She got to step 2 in 1980, and was beatified — the first layperson in America to receive that honor. Although most of her people wouldn't give her the time of day when she was alive, more than 500 Native Americans in ceremonial dress attended her beatification ceremony. The Mohawks' Lily may well become the first Native American saint.

CHAPTER
SEVEN

Early Aussies &
South Sea Self-Starters

BIG MOMMA OF PITCAIRN

The daughter of a minor Tahitian chief, MAUATEA lived the good life: eating, dancing, bathing twice a day, and getting her buttocks tattooed black. In 1789, however, a gang of smelly white men arrived in a huge canoe with sails. Always good hosts, the Tahitians offered their sexual favors to the unattractive newcomers. As a high-status woman, Mauatea drew Fletcher Christian, junior officer to Captain Bligh of the *Bounty*. The Brits were there to collect 800 breadfruit trees for the West Indies, as cheap food for the burgeoning slave trade.

Mauatea took a shine to Fletcher, and vice versa. He even got his own black-bottom tattoo, to show he cared. After six months together, the couple went through a ceremony he called "marriage".

But Fletcher had troubles at the office. On April 18, the situation erupted into a mutiny; led by Christian, the mutineers cast Bligh and others adrift in a twenty-three-foot launch. Mauatea and other Tahitians then sailed in the *Bounty* with the mutineers to set up their own paradise. Mauatea couldn't believe the miles they put on that tub. Finally, 1,350 miles later, they encountered Pitcairn Island, then burned their bridges by burning the ship.

This new place had potential; but boy would it require work. Mauatea, now called "Isabella" by Fletcher, started the matriarchal ball rolling by having the first child. She got her first taste of racism when Dad insisted on calling the baby "Thursday October" — the kind of name usually given to a slave.

Paradise Pitcairn-style quickly unraveled. Eight whites hogged most of the eleven women, and all the land. The six Polynesian males found themselves enslaved. The white mutineers were brutal — Fletcher excepted. Nevertheless, he was one of five whites murdered by disgruntled Polynesians when Mauatea was about to have her third child in 1793. Years of payback killings, promiscuity, jealousy, and alcoholism followed, disgusting Mauatea and the other women.

Eventually she married Edward Young, who thoughtfully died in 1800, leaving this South Seas Eve to spoil her kids and grandkids — including a new Thursday October Christian. (The first Thursday changed his name to Friday!)

Of the original settlers, Mauatea Christian is the one person whom today's islanders fondly recall. Among her handsome descendants on Pitcairn is Darlene Christian, whose bronzed shoulder bears a tattoo of the HMS *Bounty*, to honor Mauatea and Fletcher.

TAHITIAN DEEP THROAT

It was no luau, making a home on Pitcairn Island. JENNY ADAMS was used to Tahiti; John, her *Bounty* mutineer husband, was no prize either. Alone among the eleven women on Pitcairn, Jenny had no children. In 1794, after enduring years of spousal abuse, and mayhem that shrank the male population, she said to the other gals, "Let's leave the island!" That attempt failed; undeterred, Jenny and company conspired to wipe out the remaining whites while they slept. The mass murder bombed too. However, Tahitian grrrl power did make the men very, very nervous. After that, whenever Jenny or any of the women got fed up, they snatched up the kids and the firearms, and hid out in a remote area.

In 1817, a ship stopped at Pitcairn. Without a backward glance, Jenny Adams was aboard when it sailed. Her eyewitness account of the mutiny and the bloody happenings on Pitcairn was taken down and published in 1829. What's more, her tale has been confirmed by recent archaeology on Pitcairn.

WELCOME TO LEEP LEEP

After farming in Scotland for years, ANNE DRYSDALE said, "I canna hack this climate." Even the most rugged Scot has her health to think of — so in 1840 she emigrated Down Under, landing in the state of Victoria at Port Phillip. Upon arrival, Anne decided to homestead with CAROLINE NEWCOMB, another single woman. For twenty pounds a year, the pair could legally squat on Boronggoop, an area whose aboriginal name might mean "hair gel". Their squat was later extended to include an area with the musical name of Leep Leep.

Their wheat farming efforts were fair dinkum brilliant. In three years, the upwardly mobile squatters came back to lease more real estate. Finally the mistresses of Leep Leep were allowed to purchase and snapped up 1,357 acres, on which they built a stone house.

Anne Drysdale enjoyed thirteen years of Aussie farming before being planted herself; the township that had grown up in her area was named Drysdale in her honor. Caroline continued to run the operation, but Leep Leep just wasn't the same without Anne. Craving someone to talk to, she married a Methodist preacher. The couple rode a circuit of his ministry, coming back to the ranch at intervals. At her request, Caroline was buried in the same vault as her pioneer partner Anne.

OVERACHIEVER ON THE BOUNDING MAIN

In 1805 or thereabouts, when CH'ING YI SZAOU ("That's *Lady* Ch'ing — or die, scum!") took over the reins of her very late hubby's enterprise, she inherited 700 ships prowling the South China Sea. In a few hardworking years, Lady Ch'ing had expanded the fleet to nearly 2,000 vessels that were manned — and womanned — by the biggest gang of bloodthirsty buccaneers the world had ever seen.

Although she had no management background, the widow CEO presided over a confederation of crooks, said to have numbered 70,000, by using a variety of tactics, from a mean set of rules to generous rations of opium. She divided her fleet into six color-coordinated squadrons and gave each fleet leader a cool outfit and a title such as "Jewel of the Crew" or "Mealtime of the Frog". ("Titles are cheap," she was wont to say.) Her war council had her foster son Ch'ang P'aou as prime minister. Given the title "Steady of the Steadiest", he scored the flashy red squadron.

Being a woman herself, she ordered her pirates to eschew violence against women — a real first in the skull-and-crossbones world. When it came to rackets, however, Lady Ch'ing had an equal-opportunity policy. She ran a few nice sidelines: protection payments from terrified landlubbers along the China coast, human ransom fees, and her Lady Ch'ing garlic-water treatments (guaranteed to protect hostages from being shot).

Soon, though, instead of looting anything in its path, son Ch'ang's red squadron began fighting the green for control. The day came when the greenies managed to sink sixteen of Ch'ang's ships. Then, in a tremendous surprise move, the greenies went ashore to the governor of Macao, an independent city-state on the peninsula opposite Hong Kong. There they put in a bid for amnesty, of all things. The governor was delighted — but Lady Ch'ing was not. That move had cost her 160 fighting ships.

Was it time to wrap up the whole pirate scene? Lady Ch'ing wondered. After a quick consultation with her oracle, she too applied for on-land amnesty — and got it. To celebrate his newly pirate-free zone of Macao, the guv gave each of her hard-bitten buccaneers a jug of wine, a piece of pork, and a chunk of change as a sweetener.

For her part, Lady Ch'ing soon got her land legs. When last heard from, she had donned a smart military uniform with lots of shiny insignia and was running the hottest smuggling operation in the South China Sea.

NO VOLCANO DESCENTS REQUIRED

Her name was KAPIOLANI, and she was minding her own business as the spiritual leader of Hawaii when a boatload of pale, emaciated people showed up. The poor things were burdened with way too many black clothes — most unbecoming — but they seemed to take to her. Maybe it was because Kapiolani had the only name they could pronounce. They were hawking a new religion they called Christianity. She wasn't sure about the single deity thing, but Kapiolani did like the sound of one husband; as leader, she had a wearisome number to look after. Hawaiian male harems — they were hell.

Everyone knew you had to be in peak shape physically to be a Polynesian high priestess. Kapiolani used real peaks. In 1824, Kapiolani did a 100-mile hike, followed by a solo climb of Mauna Loa and a sizzling descent into the crater of Kilauea. And that was the easy part: she then defied the goddess Pele by refusing to make the traditional sacrifice. By now, she'd slimmed down to one god and one husband, who was screaming advice from the sidelines.

Her Hawaiian followers were impressed; the line for people signing up for Christian baptism ran halfway down the lava flow.

The white missionaries were gleeful. "But I warn you — we won't wear those outfits," new convert Kapiolani emphasized.

214

Years later, Kapiolani made good use of all her spiritual connections. She came down with breast cancer, then endured a radical mastectomy without a wisp of painkiller or happy juice. She survived it, too, a happy Amazon until her death in 1841.

AUSTRALIA'S FIRST RAGS-TO-RICHES TALE

Talk about creepy — in its new Australian penal colony, English officials decided to "improve" the male-to-female con ratio by slapping female crooks of childbearing age with seven-year sentences Down Under. That's how Esther Abrahams, a teen who'd boosted a bit of black lace, became part of the First Fleet that was headed for New South Wales in 1788. Before long, she had a male admirer — fortunately, not one of the rape-happy crew. With her looks and poise, Esther made Lt. George Johnston catch his breath (or maybe it was *hold* his breath — you wouldn't believe how fetid the ship and its humans got).

Once on shore, Esther played it coy, living with Johnston for twenty-five years before getting wed officially. In the meantime, the couple worked hard, building a family of seven and their own mansion. They even owned their own town, from bakery to blacksmith forge. From the get-go, ESTHER ABRAHAMS JOHNSTON handled the money and businesses; in time, she got big land grants of her own around Sydney. Esther was in clover. Literally. Besides growing the first clover in Australia, the couple "planted" it with the first thoroughbred stallions ever seen on the continent.

A fabulous bootstrap life: but you haven't heard the last chapter. In his will, her loving spouse left their

216

estate to Esther to manage, a gesture that caused the sons of the family to kick up something fierce. From "Unfair!" the conflict escalated to "Mom's insane!" An official contesting of the will followed, won by son Robert — and a wounded Esther went to live at a younger son's digs, easing her golden years with alcohol and memories.

BUM START, PHOTO FINISH

Having a weakness for joy-riding on someone else's horse could mean very bad news in eighteenth-century England. Mary Haydock certainly knew. Thirteen years old, a runaway, and dressed as a boy, she was caught trying to peddle a hot nag and was given the death sentence. In a sappy moment the judge relented, merely shipping Mary off to Australia for seven years of hard labor.

In October 1792, Mary landed in New South Wales. Thanks to her literacy and educated speech, she got one of the few jobs where she didn't have to work on her back: she became a nursemaid and housekeeper to the lieutenant governor's family.

It was there she met Tom Reibey, first mate for the East India Company. Despite her jailbird status, sparks flew. In 1794, Mary and the young Irishman were given permission to wed.

No honeymoon but hey, upon marriage, those seven years of servitude just vanished. The couple homesteaded a farm, started a cargo and trading business, and began a family that came to number seven kids. Mary kept the accounts and ran their store.

Reibey, always more at ease at sea than on land, began to make trading trips. On one of his voyages to India, he came home with a fever and died in 1811. A month later, his business partner keeled over. At age thirty-four, Mary had to grab all the reins of their business, which by now boasted three ships, a warehouse, several farms, a hotel, and trading clients in China, India, and elsewhere.

From Entally House, her stone mansion in Sydney, she added to her shipping line — and her bottom line — with new warehouses, vessels, and real estate. In nine years, she was looking at a fortune of 20,000 pounds! Not too shabby for an ex-con.

Time for some personal pampering, she declared, taking two of her daughters with her to England. Erk — she'd forgotten how cold, damp, and socially cramped the place was.

In 1821 she returned to her Aussie home, a move she hoped would erase her first, fettered arrival as a teenaged convict. Deciding that she kinda liked being single, Mary remained that way. At age fifty-one, she was able to retire and continue her good works. Besides giving to charities, she took an active role in education as one of the governors of the Free Grammar School.

Even at this stage, Aussie society remained cruelly snobbish. To the end of her life, Mary wore the "convict taint". Nevertheless, she forged ahead, and saw that her children married well — to society snobs, of course.

In a final triumph over her humble beginnings, MARY HAYDOCK REIBEY was honored by her adoptive country in a special way: her droll and spectacled likeness appears on the Australian $20 bill. A photo finish for a mighty dark horse.

TASMANIANS' LAST STAND

Until 1800, aboriginal leaders like TRUGANINI were still living tranquil lives on Tasmania (turn south at Australia, can't miss it). Her Palawah people had been on these islands for 30,000 years, give or take a millennium. So when they first heard the words, "G'day mate, which way's the barbie?" they didn't get too excited.

Soon, however, whites, most of them brutal convicts, were all over the place. Truganini saw her mom murdered by whalers, her sister abducted and shot by sealers. She herself was raped. Finally, Truganini and her dad, accompanied by the endangered tatters of their tribe, fled deep into the bush.

In 1830, the natives got a break. Maybe. Aussie headquarters sent George Robinson, "Protector of the Aborigines", on a mission to find the last 300 Palawahs. Robinson collared Truganini, saying, "We respect your way of life so much, we're gonna dump you — er, protect you — on Flinders Island; it'll be fabulous!"

It took five years of fast talk for Truganini and her new husband Woorrady to smoke out the aborigines in hiding and emigrate to the settlement of Wybalenna on Flinders. (The more hostile natives called them "the decoy blacks".) During that time, she kept Robinson's hide free of hostile spears — even saved the guy from drowning. She shoulda let him sink.

220

Once the aborigines had been taken off Tasmania, George insisted on teaching them European customs. The Sunday school thing was bad enough. But those English canned peas — ugh! Tiny, resource-scarce Flinders became a prison camp, an island exile where most sickened and died.

When Truganini finally saw through white fairy-tales, it was too late. All but forty-six expired on Flinders Island. She and a small band escaped the island for a time, killing a handful of white men before being recaptured. Ultimately, in 1847, Truganini and the pitiful remnants of her people were returned to their badly trashed mainland territory around Oyster Cove. For the rest of her life, Truganini hunted in the bush, collected husbands and seafood, and visited the places sacred to her. As the others of her culture died off, she became a local "character" — a token abo.

Whites didn't even honor her last wish; instead of burial behind the mountains, she got a grave in the women's penitentiary — only to be exhumed in skeletal form and placed as a tourist attraction in Hobart Museum, where she hung until 1947. Some years later, Truganini's ashes were finally and fittingly scattered upon the waters off Tasmanian tribal land.

AUSTRALIA'S BAAAH HUMBUG

Her maiden name was Veale, but ELIZABETH MACARTHUR would become fond of mutton. Very fond. An overeducated Aussie pioneer, she was hip-deep in sheep. The sheep were also newcomers — Elizabeth and her army officer husband John imported the merinos from Spain.

In 1790, the couple homesteaded a place at Parramatta, near Sydney in New South Wales, named it Elizabeth Farm, and set about raising the ratio of whites to aborigines by having babies. Seven survived childhood. In between farming, dairying, and her own breeding experiences, Elizabeth conducted breeding experiments with the sheep — and gave birth to the wool export industry.

Meanwhile, her quarrelsome, suspicious husband kept getting sidetracked in duels, rum rebellions, and other white-collar crimes. Eventually, he was court-martialed in England and served an eight-year exile, which annoyed Elizabeth no end. No help around the ranch — just when things were getting off the ground! Luckily she had ninety cons and ex-cons to draw from. With their labor, Mrs. Macarthur increased her flocks from 1,000 to more than 4,000.

About now, it was time to send the three oldest kids to England for school. Once he'd finished up his exile, her husband kindly offered to stay on, so he could take the kids on holiday breaks, and oh yes, peddle the Macarthur wool on the European market.

Elizabeth, meanwhile, continued the backbreaking work of a major stock operation, from shearing to slaughtering. She kept on experimenting to improve the wool and the farm itself. Now and then, she'd get a letter from John (by now, she wasn't all that clear what he looked like), bubbling about the latest outing he and the kids had taken, and throwing in a bit of stilted praise to keep her motivated: "I cannot express how much I am pleased at the account you give of the state of our affairs under your excellent and prudent management . . ."

In 1816, one other male recognized Elizabeth's hard work. The Governor of New South Wales awarded the forty-nine-year-old 600 acres near Camden "in recognition of your work toward the improvement of agriculture". Four years later, the Macarthurs were the biggest land barons in the province.

Elizabeth outlived her mostly absent, later full-on manic-depressive husband by seventeen years — ample time to hear others warble the praises of "John Macarthur, father of the Australian wool industry". Baaah humbug!

ROLLING STONE DOWN UNDER

Londoner Jane Griffin didn't become LADY JANE FRANKLIN until she hit thirty-seven. New husband John, whose passion was Arctic exploration, had nearly died of starvation in his 1819 search for the Northwest Passage. After he and Jane got hitched, he was "rewarded" for his sub-zero efforts by a grateful British government.

"Darling," he reported, "They've given me a post as lieutenant governor!"

"Lovely. Where, dear?"

"Er . . . Van Diemen's Land." It took a while just to find anyone who knew where that was. Lady Jane found herself on a slow boat to Australia, then south to Tasmania, aka the convict colony of Van Diemen's. A bit wary of what passed for "society" in Tasmania, Jane went the high road and founded the first Royal Society for the Advancement of Science outside England. Later, she threw together financing for a Museum of Natural History and Botanical Gardens.

Jane cheered up when she finally got a female visitor: ELIZABETH GOULD, there with her publisher husband to paint birds. With Elizabeth staying at Jane's comfortable government house during the winter of 1839, the two got in some great girl talk, while Elizabeth cranked out seventy-four watercolors of local plants.

Once the Goulds left, Jane went back to exploring Tasmania, founding things, and pushing for social reform. She fought hard to bring about better living conditions for the female convict population, but was shouted down in the press.

Tired of political infighting, Lady Jane pointed her riding crop and restless spirit toward adventure travel. Among her female firsts: riding overland from Melbourne to Sydney and climbing 4,166-foot Mt. Wellington, the highest peak in Tasmania.

In due course, John lost his post and the couple returned to England, where John succeeded in mounting another Arctic expedition. In May 1845, Jane waved good-bye to him and two shipsful of men. None was ever seen alive again. Various rescue expeditions got underway; all fizzled. Disgusted at the lack of follow-through, Jane privately funded another expedition in 1858. It found (1) a definitively dead husband, and (2) his undeniable discovery of the Northwest Passage.

Jane herself continued to sedately raise hell in England, writing journals and taking trips until her eighty-fourth year.

TASMANIA'S AMAZON

Embarrassing moment number one in WALYER's life: as a teen in old Tasmania, she was kidnapped by a rival aborigine group and traded to some scummy white sealers — for a couple of dogs and some flour! In 1828, she managed to escape her captors and get back to her people. Bright note: She grabbed a gun or two before departure and immediately taught her clan of nine men and one woman how to use firearms. Before long, whites from Australia to Tasmania were uneasily calling her "the Amazon". Besides leading an aggressive band of aborigines and killing every white she could, she warned many other groups on the island of the fate that faced native people. Alone among aborigine women — and men — cunning Walyer had the motivation and the farsightedness to fight the invading European culture in an organized fashion. Not that it got her very far; captured and jailed in early 1831, valiant Walyer died a few months later, on June 5.

AUSSIE APPLESEED

By the 1830s, Australia desperately needed some emigrants with clean criminal records and a knack for growing things. When the recruiters hit Sussex, England, a couple of pioneer types, MARIA ANN SMITH and her husband Tom, signed on. After their arrival, laden with seeds, cuttings, and five children, the Smiths made their way to Ryde, whose microclimate proved ideal for growing fruit. An experimenter to the core, Maria Ann fiddled with crab apples from Tasmania — only to find much later that a seed or an apple she'd thrown away had sprouted a tree by the creek. The sport, or fixed mutation, it bore was a crisp and juicy green apple that turned out to be marvelous for cooking and eating raw. By now a grandma, Maria got an apple named "Granny Smith" in her honor. Australia got a marvelous new export. And the world gained a toothsome new "granny".

CALAMITY CONQUEROR

MARGARET CATCHPOLE's first job was as housemaid to the Cobbolds in Suffolk, England. Pretty hum-drum, really. Then Margaret got a boyfriend to die for — a local smuggler. He persuaded the young housemaid that his career would really take off if she would steal a horse for him. As any bloke knew, smuggling on foot was so uncool.

Untrained in horse-napping but willing to learn, Margaret nabbed a fine mount — but was soon hobbled by her new status as horse thief. Oops, her smuggler sweetie had forgotten to mention that horse theft carried the death penalty (but what didn't, in those days).

Faced with the distinct possibility of a noose, Margaret escaped capture several times, once eluding the authorities by disguising herself as a sailor on a warship. Finally, tiring of Catchpole's slipperiness, English authorities deported her to Australia. She arrived at the shores of New South Wales on the good convict ship *Nile*, December 14, 1801. Merry Christmas.

Early Australia was a human dumping ground; its huge and predatory male convict population and the resulting danger for women shocked even Margaret, who by now had seen something of the seamier side of life. She wrote to her aunt and uncle in England, "I pray to God to keep you all from such a wicked country as this."

Nevertheless, flexible Margaret found work — some of it even legal! — as a midwife, a nurse, and later, a storekeeper. Her adventures in and around Sydney were many.

Catchpole, who lived to a great age, never married. She survived such calamities as the great flood in 1806, which she rode out perched on the top of a house. Later she accumulated a bit of material wealth, and to her own surprise, became a humanitarian.

As one of the more than 3,000 women who were sent to Australia as convicts, Catchpole stood out because she was literate. From a historian's standpoint, she's priceless. Margaret's letters to family and friends in England have given the world a most unusual look at Australia's early years.

BYE, BYE, BIRDIE

An English governess when she collided with a self-taught taxidermist and avid avian fan, ELIZABETH COXEN GOULD probably met her future mate John at the London Zoo, where he became curator in 1829.

After marriage, the Goulds jumped into publishing. Flora and fauna were huge; ditto, books on natural history. Their first title, lavishly illustrated, was *A Century of Birds from the Himalayan Mountains*. From John's rough sketches, Elizabeth painted watercolors of 100 species, then transferred the images to lithographic blocks. Other artists hand-colored the lithos to match her originals.

Gould presold subscriptions for their work, to finance the costly process. Like a man possessed, John produced book after book. Like a woman possessed, Elizabeth produced painting after painting — and child after child.

The Goulds' most triumphant collaborations were their tomes on birds and mammals of Australia, for which Mrs. G got out of the birth chamber and into the bush. Leaving grandparents to cope with the babies, in May 1838 the Goulds took a four-month trip to Australia, then spent two years there gathering material. Much of the time, Elizabeth lived in a bush camp, painting daily, while trying to keep the more toxic fauna from devouring the kids they'd brought.

230

However, she was unable to persuade John to keep his fly buttoned — in 1840 she gave birth to her seventh.

Did multi-motherhood slacken the artistic pace? Quite the reverse. John, whose enthusiasm for birds extended to eating them (he often downed a dozen parakeets at a sitting), kept that brush in his wife's hand. *The Birds of Australia*, a seven-volume opus, contained 600 color plates by Elizabeth; *The Synopsis* (a paperback version), 73 plates. Elizabeth also did books on toucans and assisted with a book of finches and other birds that illustrated Charles Darwin's work in the Galapagos Islands.

One year after leaving Australia, Elizabeth had baby number eight. Then a fatal case of childbed fever hit — giving her the first rest she'd had in years.

John missed her dreadfully; before he ate them all, he even named a colored finch for her: *Amadina gouldiae*. He went on to publish fourteen books containing nearly 3,000 paintings — many of them Elizabeth's. She got little or no credit; today she's a footnote, her oeuvre as a painter invariably chalked up to John Gould.

EARLY ABORIGINE AFICIONADA

A delicate blonde from a veddy well-bred English family, Georgiana Kennedy had been serious about botanizing since she was a child. At twenty-four she fell in love with "Handsome Jack" Molloy, who proposed marriage — and emigration to Western Australia.

The bride-to-be packed her trousseau, some seeds and bulbs, and went off to have her hair done — little realizing it was the *very last time* she would ever get a comb-out or see a conditioner. (Makes your skin crawl, doesn't it?)

Drawn by Aussie land grants that promised "Easy Wealth! Good pasture! No beasts of prey or loathsome reptiles!" the greenhorn newlyweds attempted to homestead one hellish place after another. GEORGIANA MOLLOY had to move, set up a household in a canvas tent, and replant a garden three times. Her other chores included running a dairy, harvesting the wheat crop, birthing seven babies, and making kangaroo tail soup and cockatoo pie without servants, who'd run off after seeing what drudgery life in the bush was.

Perpetual motion Molloy still found time to befriend the Nyungar people, learn their aboriginal tongue — and win many of their medicinal plant and herbal secrets. When she asked, "Got any good scurvy recipes?" they even introduced her to rock spinach and pigweed. She scrupulously recorded their lore on

232

paper; with their expertise, her seed and plant collection grew, as did her reputation.

In 1838, a playboy botanist called Captain Mangles wrote Georgiana, asking if she'd do a spot of seed collecting. No pay, mind you, and no recognition either, although male botanists in England and America were later delighted to share — and publish as their own — her data on Aussie flora. Still, her research gave deep meaning to Georgiana's life and helped her through physical hardships and traumas, including the deaths of several of her children.

When this brilliant botanist of the bush herself died of postpartum complications at age thirty-seven, one of her horticultural admirers in Britain eulogized, "Not one in ten thousand who go out into distant lands has done what she did for gardens . . ." A sweetly scented flower, as tall and slim as Georgiana, was named *Boronia molloyae* in her honor.

CHAPTER
EIGHT

Headline Makers
& Risk-Takers

THE OTHER POCAHONTAS

Want to win a bar bet? Just ask anyone who the "Oklahoma Pocahontas" was.

Three-quarters Creek, MILLY FRANCIS was born and raised in Florida when the place was just a large swampy area to the south of the fledgling United States of America. Like their Seminole neighbors, the Creeks often made raids on white settlements, trying to make spare change by taking captives and ransoming them. One day in 1817, Milly heard Seminole warriors making a racket over a particularly good catch.

Indeed it was: Captain McKrimmon of the U.S. Army. The Seminoles were all set to kill him; suavely, Milly talked them into letting her have the captain, then bunked him with her tribe while they put out the word they were soliciting offers.

After saving him from extinction, she and the Creeks sold McKrimmon to the Spaniards, the high bidders this round. Milly might not have thought any more about it, except that a year or so later, the captain showed up at her camp. He'd been duly ransomed from the Spaniards and now he was back with a proposal. A marriage proposal. Milly was flabbergasted. I mean, nice uniform and all, but that ghostly skin, that body hair, those blue eyes! Sick.

She turned him down. Nicely. After all, she had wedding plans with a Native American from Georgia. Well, that was a disaster. She was barely wed when all Five Civilized Tribes — the Creeks, Cherokees, Chickasaws, Choctaws, and Seminoles — got to shuffle off to Oklahoma, on the forced march known as the "Trail of Tears".

Stuck, broke, and sick in Oklahoma, Milly struggled to survive. Her husband was a goner with tuberculosis; she had the disease as well.

Just then, an Army major happened by their wretched dwelling and sat down to chat. Strangely moved by Milly's tale of saving a U.S. Army captain and the troubles that had befallen her and the Five Tribes, the officer went to bat for her when he returned to Washington, D.C.

Hooray! A conscience-ridden Congress voted to send Milly Francis a pension and a thank-you medal. Wouldn't you know, though, thanks to that breakneck Congressional pace, the darn thing arrived too late. The "Oklahoma Pocahontas" died before the funds could do a bit of good.

CAPTURED BY INDIANS? OR RESCUED?

Born into a preacher's clan — the leading family of Deerfield, Massachusetts — EUNICE WILLIAMS led a privileged life until she was eight. Then, in a terrifying raid by Iroquois Mohawks, she, her family, and nearly a hundred neighbors were captured in 1704. Her mother died on the trek north to French Canada; her father and brother were ransomed, then tried for years to ransom Eunice.

All their efforts failed. Finally the Williamses learned the uncomfortable truth: Eunice herself didn't want to come back. Adopted by the tribe, she forgot English, married a Mohawk, and had several daughters. Perhaps the most ghastly part of the story, from the Puritan point of view, was the fact that she had adopted Catholicism, too.

Eunice came to embrace the life of two adoptive cultures, Native American and French Catholic. Affectionately called by her Indian nickname, "she brings in corn", she stood as godmother to both whites and Iroquois. She saw her daughters Marie and Catherine marry local chieftains, and lived to be eighty-nine.

The story of this unredeemed captive is fascinating for several reasons. During the United States' first 200 years, many females besides Eunice were kidnapped by Indians — and refused to return to their own families and cultures. It's a penetrating and little-explored commentary on the role that women played — or were kept from playing — in white colonial society.

DOUBLE-LATTE LEADER

She didn't need to open any coffeehouses; energetic MARY COFFIN STARBUCK generated her own caffeine. An awed English visitor described Nantucket Island's leading citizen and politico in 1701: "The islanders esteem her as a judge among them, for little is done without her." Mary came to the island with her folks, Tristam and Dionis Coffin, who, unlike some whites we could mention, actually bought the place from indigenous people before developing it. As a teen, Mary ran a general store, selling everything from shoes to beef; she often got paid in fish, the island "currency". (No record as to how she made change — sardines perhaps?)

After marrying a wealthy farmer named Starbuck, she had ten children, while continuing to dominate politics. So much business was transacted at her place, it was nicknamed "Parliament House". Mrs. Starbuck starred in local debates, often prefacing her remarks with, "My husband and I think . . ."

When this mover and shaker decided to abandon the Puritan religion for Quakerism, she made sure that everyone on the island had the same opportunity. Or else. By her death in 1717, you'd better believe that Nantucket was a Quaker headquarters.

A GLORIOUS BARGAIN

MARY YOUNG PICKERSGILL didn't plan on becoming a flag maker. But then, she didn't plan on becoming a widow, either. An expert seamstress, Mary often worked with her mother Rebecca on sewing commissions in Baltimore. In 1813, someone knocked at Mary's door; it was the commander of nearby Fort McHenry with a proposal. Not marital — financial. The country was at war with the British — again. As he explained, "We want two flags. A smaller flag for everyday use, and a really big sucker — one that those (expletive deleted) Brits can see at a distance."

A patriotic sort, Mary didn't even charge a deposit, but set to work. Muttering "You want big? I'll give you big," she created a beautiful red-white-and-blue banner forty-two feet long and thirty feet wide, each of the fifteen stars on it measuring two feet from point to point. Since both flags had to be sewn by hand, Mary's mom and others got in on the action. Sewing about 1.7 million stitches, it's now thought.

By the next summer, Mary's creations were riding the breeze over Fort McHenry. In September, the British made things really breezy by launching a savage attack on the fort. An ammunition-allergic lawyer named Francis Scott Key happened to be in a boat on the river, and watched the whole hairy battle. What with all the artillery going off, the air got so smoky that

Key couldn't even see the fort. When the smoke cleared, there was one of Mary's flags, still flying high. Key was so goose-bumped that he composed a poem called "The Star-Spangled Banner" in mid-stream. The lyrics became the country's national anthem — and Mary's larger flag became known as Old Glory.

You can still see Old Glory (recently spiffed up, albeit only four-fifths of its original glorious self, thanks to earlier souvenir paring) in Washington, D.C. Another poignant souvenir from patriot and businesswoman Pickersgill's life is displayed at her Star-Spangled Banner Flag House in Baltimore: her $405.90 invoice for Old Glory's creation. Quite a bargain, compared to your average Pentagon purchase.

LUCKY IN HISTORY, UNLUCKY IN LOVE

BETSY ROSS, the subject of one of our gooier tall tales, had a long moniker by the time she reached Social Security age (not that there *was* any back then). Born Elizabeth Griscom, she was by turns Mrs. Ross, Ashburn, and Claypoole.

This good Philly dame, born a Quaker on January 1, 1752, got drummed out of her church when she married an Anglican upholsterer named John Ross. He died in the militia two years later, but at least she'd learned a trade. Now an upholsterer ("We can also make your flags and banners"), Betsy fought to return to the religious fold — and found a home with an oxymoronic sect called "the Fighting Quakers".

She barely had time to produce a son and daughter with her next spouse before he was captured and died in an English prison. With husband number three, John Claypoole, Betsy had five daughters before he became paralyzed (he lingered until 1817).

For most of her eighty-four years, Betsy valiantly carried on as caregiver, breadwinner, and parent, supporting herself by sewing. In 1777, she did whip up a couple of flags for the Philadelphia Navy, but there's no evidence that she made the first U.S. flag at George Washington's behest — or anyone's. No secret shopping trips to her upholstery shop by the congressional committee, either.

241

The whole warm and fuzzy story was concocted by her grandson Bill Canby, at the 1876 national centennial. In a speech, Bill asserted that his granny had made the first flag, and had told him about it on her deathbed forty years earlier. Even then, most people didn't buy it.

But the nation was about to celebrate its hundredth birthday, and needed some heartwarming history — fast. A Betsy Ross memorial association sprang up, soon selling a cool 2 million memberships at a dime each. In 1890, painter Charles Weisberger did a huge canvas of Betsy Ross showing her creation to the congressional committee. With this momentum, the myth took flight, finding its way like a computer virus into textbooks and women's histories. Betsy *was* extraordinary, but not in the way she's been labeled.

Aztec Eyewitness News

Montezuma, the trustingly dippy ruler of old Mexico before Spanish conquistador Hernán Cortés steam-rollered him, had a brighter brother named Cuitlahuac. He in turn had an erudite daughter whose Aztec name we no longer know — she was baptized MARÍA BARTOLA by the victors. She lived through the terrible times when the Spanish first won Tenochtitlán, the ancient capital (now Mexico City). When Montezuma bit the dust, Cuitlahuac took over. About ten minutes into his tenure, the Europeans' secret weapon (they called it "smallpox") hit. Cuitlahuac died of it.

By then, María was out of town, sitting on the throne of nearby Ixtapalapa. A studious and thoughtful person, she was literate in both Nahautl, the Aztec tongue, and Spanish. From her father, she'd inherited a legacy of priceless pictographic works, called *codexes*, of the Aztec people. From these resources, and her own firsthand research on battle sites (sometimes while the fight was still raging), she began to write a history of her times.

As if the lives lost and the culture destroyed weren't bad enough, María Bartola's historical work — the first of its kind — was later burned by the Spaniards. We only know of it, and her, thanks to a later historian named Fernando de Alva Ixtlixochitl — whose name shows that he was of mixed Aztec and Spanish blood.

243

To date, Fernando's raves about Bartola's ability and writing are the only trace left of this bold Aztec eyewitness to history.

AN EARLY RISER

A Quaker like the rest of her farming family, JEMIMA WILKINSON came down to breakfast one morning and announced that she'd died in the night. Not to worry, she added, she'd been reborn as the new Messiah. Pass the oatmeal, please.

Jemima, a commanding figure who wore kilts and a hat that made her even taller, had received divine marching orders. Her assignments: Found a new church and gather a flock, then prepare them for the Second Coming, an event that would occur in her lifetime. That is, her second lifetime. Whatever.

Beginning in 1776, Messiah Wilkinson spread the word, slowly gathering some 250 converts from Rhode Island, Connecticut, Pennsylvania, and Massachusetts. She led her group, called "the Universal Friends", to New York, where they founded a settlement named Jerusalem in the Finger Lakes region. Since the Second Coming was imminent, no one worried too much about the future of the Universal Friends — which was good, since Wilkinson had established a strict "No canoodling" policy among the faithful.

In addition to her ideas about celibacy and her belief in the Golden Rule, this fem Messiah had an enlightened attitude toward Indians. She and her followers actually made friends with the ones dwelling in the area. Thanks to that charitable act, the colony prospered until Messiah Wilkinson's second (or third) death in 1820.

Although disappointed that Armageddon was seriously behind schedule, Jemima left precise postmortem instructions. To facilitate her rebirth, the Universal Friends were to leave her body above ground. So there they sat, until finally the stench of an all-too-decomposing Jemima drove the last gagging Friend away.

In 1876, just 100 years after Jemima had begun her Messianic quest, the last of her followers died — in the traditional way, we might add.

SATANIC SLEEPOVER, ANYONE?

Old TITUBA, the Parris household slave, missed her Caribbean homeland during the frosty winters in Salem village. When her chores were done, Tituba played for hours with Abigail and Betty, the children in the Parris household. Gradually, other neighborhood girls, mostly bored teenagers, were drawn to the cozy kitchen — to listen to Tituba, whose Barbados tales included fortunetelling and bits of voodoo.

This group of eight dabbled in small sorceries, from palm reading to conjuring with scissors and a candle. Some, like ANN PUTNAM, a high-strung twelve-year-old, dabbled more deeply. She believed her sister had been hounded to death and wanted to make contact with her spirit.

These goings-on with Tituba remained secret for months. But the stress of doing what was a deadly sin in the eyes of Puritan grownups made the smallest girls sick. Their hysterics, babbling in tongues, and convulsions quickly spread to the other girls. Some became physically ill; others appeared psychotic.

Salem villagers were appalled. Charges began flying faster than a Black Mass-bound broomstick. Preacher Parris led the witchcraft push. The supposedly bewitched girls became spiritual bloodhounds. Most gave testimony in court; Ann Putnam was especially verbal.

When it came time to testify, Tituba said what everyone most wanted — and feared — to hear. There were red cats and red rats that talked to her, she said. There was a tall man, and strange shapes that wanted her to pinch the children.

Dozens of Massachusetts women — from Tituba to a hard-of-hearing grandma named Rebecca Nurse to a beggar named Sarah Good — were accused and convicted of witchcraft. In 1692, twenty were hanged.

Tituba, meanwhile, sat on death row for thirteen months. The following year, she and the others still locked up were finally released. The witch craze in Salem was thankfully dead.

One slight personal problem: Tituba was hit with a large bill for jailhouse grub and her cell nights. The court being unwilling to accept her "Gosh, I was sorta busy, behind bars," Tituba was sold at a slave auction to pay for her hoosegow B&B.

MERCIFULLY SHORT FAME

MERCY SHORT couldn't believe the bummers in her life. Let's see, there was her capture by Indians, who'd made her walk from New Hampshire to Canada. She'd witnessed the butchery of her parents and other family members. Even after she was ransomed, she got no praise, no glory, not even an NPR interview. At seventeen, she was an orphan in Boston with a crummy job as a housemaid.

Then, on her day off, she went to Boston Prison to visit a friend. Well OK, she went to peek at the accused Salem witches, like everyone else. While she was there, one of the witches, SARAH GOOD, asked her for tobacco. Mercy made loud fun of her. From that day on, Mercy suffered from diabolical visions.

Even after hapless Sarah was hanged, Mercy continued to have visits from specters. With her descriptions of "a short tawny man, with One Cloven Foot", she had religious bigwig Cotton Mather, a keen student of psychology, hanging on every word. In December, Mercy fell into major convulsions during one of Mather's sermons. (Given the length of his sermons, who wouldn't?)

What with the congregation praying over her, her devil-induced fits and fasts, and the coming and going of "witches' marks" on her body, Mercy was pretty busy — and the center of Bostonian attention until the

249

spring of 1693. More than a year after the Salem trial, she came out of her trance. While Mather and his congregation were busy congratulating themselves, Mercy took up more mundane activities, like bar-hopping and fornicating. (You'd think they would have stepped up the prayer vigils. But no.) Mercy Short's strange time in the limelight was over.

The Women Behind "Molly Pitcher"

Like "G. I. Joe", "Molly Pitcher" became a generic nickname given to a number of gutsy Revolutionary War heroines. They represented woman at her finest. Or at her wit's end. These women of humble backgrounds saw far more action than hauling pitchers of H_2O to cool cannon barrels and to revive parched troops.

The earliest documented "pitcher" on the mound was MARGARET CORBIN. During the Battle of Fort Washington on Manhattan Island, this twenty-five-year-old aided her husband John, a private in the Pennsylvania artillery corps. As the Hessian soldiers blasted away, Margaret swabbed out Big Bertha between firings (a tidy cannon is a functioning cannon, she'd been told), and helped John ram in the next ball. At length, the enemy scored a fatal slam-dunk on John, whereupon Margaret took over his fieldpiece until she, too, was riddled by hostile fire.

Three years after the battle on November 16, 1776, and now assigned to the Invalid Regiment at West Point with one arm permanently useless, "Captain Molly" was awarded the first military pension given to a woman. (Other female vets would wait up to forty years to receive theirs!) Corbin's award? Disability pay for life (though half what a disabled male received). Plus other perks: a set of clothes and a monthly ration of liquor. Wow! Overwhelmed by their generosity,

Corbin didn't start squawking to the brass until it became clear that she couldn't collect — the PX refused to issue booze to females! In 1782, she submitted a "bill" for 257 gills of whiskey, the amount now due her. After yet another long wait, she finally got the all-clear — and a formidable cache of bottles.

The toughest challenge Corbin faced, however, was living on her miserable pension. Military folks who knew her helped out with blankets and such. Wearing a raunchy old Army coat, Margaret augmented her diet by fishing off the docks until her death at fifty in 1800. By then she was slightly batty, a vet who insisted on being saluted as "Captain Molly". (We'd be cranky too, in her situation.) Her burial was obscure. In 1926, she was reburied with honors by the DAR at the West Point cemetery.

Another "Molly Pitcher" with multiple versions to her story was Pennsylvanian MARY LUDWIG HAYS MCCAULEY, a tobacco-chewing trouper of a trooper who saw action at the Battle of Monmouth, New Jersey, in 1778. On that long, hot June day, Mary helped her husband William load his cannon. Supposedly pregnant at the time, this twentysomething had nerve. An amazed eyewitness saw a British cannonball pass between her legs, ripping away the bottom half of her garments. Mary blithely returned fire, saying, "Lucky for me the thing didn't carry off something I really valued!" When William took a bullet, Mary jumped in to take over cannon duty.

After the war, Mary had a son and went through two husbands. In 1822, she finally got a $40 annual pension out of the government. For years, she lived at the Carlisle post, cooking for the soldiers. She grew stout and ruddy of face, fond of reliving battles with anyone who would listen, until her death on January 22, 1832.

99.9 PERCENT PURE

It was bad enough, being put on trial as a witch. Which she wasn't. But GRACE SHERWOOD could never remember the sink-or-float sorcery test. Which one showed you were innocent? On July 10, 1706, she got to find out. Trussed up and tossed into the Lynnhaven River by a Virginia court, a gasping Grace bobbed to the surface. Guilty! Came the gloating cry from the riverbanks. Then local matrons ran a crone scan on her — where every mole or wart counted. Despite a "witch mark" or two, and her Ivory-soap performance in the river, Grace got off. A hung jury? Admiration of her swimming stroke? We'll never know. Sherwood died of natural causes thirty-six years later — one of the few happy outcomes of the "devil made her do it" craze in America. You can still take a plunge at Witch Duck Point in Virginia Beach; unlike Grace, you don't need to be tied up.

LET THE GOOD TIMES ROLL

For years, southern Louisiana had plenty of 'gators but almost no girls. The few females on hand were Ursuline nuns or exceptions like MADAME LANGLOIS, the gifted cook and housekeeper to Jean Baptiste Bienville, the governor of the Louisiana colony.

In 1704, the area received a shipment of cassettes that would change everything. The cassettes in question were *petites cassettes* or small dowry trunks belonging to two dozen French teens from Acadia (now Canadian Nova Scotia). "Hot dawg!" cried local men, hungry for home cookin' and warm bodies that didn't have hair all over them.

However, the "casket girls", as they came to be known, soon expressed their un-delight with Louisiana. Swamps — they were not *jolies*. And the cuisine — *quelle horreur!* Even though they couldn't return to their homeland (now captured by the Brits), the casket girls were about to walk when Madame Langlois jumped into the breach.

Over the years, Langlois had learned to cook with local ingredients. She'd borrowed recipes from slaves and sniffed out the culinary secrets of local Choctaw Indians. Nobly, she was willing to share. Madame showed the girls how to make such dishes as "gumbo", from crawdads, crab, an exotic veggie called okra, peppers, and filé, or sassafras powder. Soon she had the casket girls whipping up hominy, grits, and cornbread for all they were worth. Louisiana men (at least, several dozen of them) finally got a social life — and the world got Cajun food.

But, as the guv said to Madame Langlois, a handful of casket girls wasn't going to cut it, colonization-wise. He kept bugging King Louis XIV of France for more women. A royal cheapskate, good old *"l'état, c'est moi"* Louie saw a nifty way to recycle the female dregs of French society. In 1719, he sent the first batch of what would eventually total thousands of women. Unlike the middle-class, convent-educated casket girls, most of these cruelly treated deportees had been in Paris prisons for real or supposed crimes.

Although many died en route or shortly thereafter, many women survived to make a new life in the muddy, mosquito-ridden settlement of New Orleans. Today you'll hear Big Easy locals brag about their "casket girl" ancestors — but you'd be hard-pressed to find anyone who claims to be descended from one of the valiant deportees.

SO WHAT'S WRONG WITH "COLDENIA"?

Educated in part by her learning-loving mother Alice, JANE COLDEN grew up on a fancy estate in the colony of New York. From her Scottish dad Cadwallader, she got a library imported from England — and a fanatical enthusiasm for botany. By her teens, she was corresponding with the leading naturalists of the day, including Linnaeus himself. (When it came to answering her mail, though, Daddy stepped in. After all, her correspondence was about sex — even if they were discussing plants.)

A pity Jane's dad didn't think women were "capable" of learning those nasty Latin names. Jane soldiered on anyway, mastering the Linnaean classification system. By 1757, she'd collected specimens of more than 300 regional plant species, cataloged them, and made precise sketches and ink impressions. One standout was a scented creamy white beauty of a flower from a glossy-leaved bush she'd discovered. That same year, she produced a catalog of New York flora. In 1759, she wrote to the Edinburgh Philosophical Society in Scotland about her sweet-smelling findings. No reply.

Meanwhile Jane wed a doctor named Farquhar, had a son, and moved to New York City — then quietly died on the vine at forty-two.

Four years later, the Philosophical Society got around to publishing Jane's description of the gardenia genus in their journal. However, a Scottish botanist named Alexander Garden was given credit for Jane's flower find — and it was called "gardenia" in his honor. Rather than giving Colden her due, he smirked that her work was "extremely accurate". (What was *with* those glory-grabbing Scots?)

Years after she herself was planted, Jane Colden got recognition as an important physical scientist of the New World; her essays and observations on plants still reside at the Edinburgh Philosophical Society.

SINGLE WITH REAL ESTATE? GOTTA BE DIABOLICAL!

No one to ask if she could buy this or that; no husband to appease, feed, or gratify sexually. KATHERINE HARRISON had to admit it: she was enjoying her new widowhood. A very solvent resident of Wethersfield, Massachusetts, Katherine made good use of her valuable farmland, raising cattle and growing corn. With no sons, brothers, or male relatives to butt in, she did what she pleased.

What she didn't do was remarry. Not only did the macho city fathers and Katherine's farmer neighbors find this offensive; they found it downright . . . irresistible.

Somewhere, perhaps at a late-night bull session, someone had a bright idea. "Let's accuse Harrison of being a witch, then confiscate her property!" The Puritan equivalent of high fives all around.

Soon the rumor mill was rolling. Mrs. Harrison's kind deeds — attending sick neighbors, for instance — got transformed into something sinister. Instead of being recognized as a healer, she was accused of practicing magic. Her ability to tell fortunes? Clearly a diabolical trait.

On her farm, Katherine began to find dead heifers and cattle. Something broke the back of her steer. She found one of her cows with a hole drilled into its side.

Alien drive-by? More like malicious neighbors, Katherine surmised. The vandalism escalated. Her crops, from hops to corn, were destroyed.

Katherine angrily reported the attacks to the local court. Not only did they refuse to give her any help — they airily fined her. "Bringing false witness", they called it. Katherine offered to bring in the cow with the drill-hole in it, but they weren't having any.

Eventually, the town's vicious plan of attack worked. Labeled a "witch" by the community, fearful of being tried as one, and unable to get legal recourse, Katherine was hounded out of Wethersfield, leaving her rich farmlands behind. Case closed.

Harrison's case is yet another example of the real motives behind many accusations of witchcraft: economics. Modern researchers have found that male colonists, especially those in New England, were land-crazy and obsessed with owning as much of it as possible. When it came to seventeenth-century real estate, apparently, a Puritan male could use fair means or foul.

TRY SQUISHING A MILE
IN HER MOCCASINS

Her face now adorns a $1 coin, and it's about time SACAGAWEA the Bird Woman got her mug on something. At sixteen she triumphed as an interpreter, guide, negotiator, native pacifier, and food forager — all while carrying her new infant.

When Lemhi Shoshone joined the U.S. Army expedition launched by Lewis and Clark, she'd already endured kidnap, enslavement, spousal abuse, her trapper husband's lack of hygiene, and being called "squaw" or "hey you" by everyone.

But that sloggy, soggy trip from North Dakota to the Pacific Coast was a real nightmare. And Fort Clatsop, where they wintered, was even worse. True, on November 24, 1805, she *had* gotten to vote on where the camp should be. None of the great white hunters saw it her way, though. Sigh. Men.

For months, Sacagawea had heard about "the ocean". Naturally, she developed a yen to see that big puddle of salt water. Clark obnoxiously tried to ace her out of her only trip to the beach — and a chance to see the monstrous *ecola* fish washed up there! She got in Clark's face, and got her husband to support her. For once.

It was quite a walk; she carried baby Pompey up and down a mountain, then south to Tillamook Head. The

261

ocean was better than she'd hoped; who knew water could behave like that? And the monster! (Clark called it a 105-foot whale.) By the time they got there, though, locals had cleaned the *ecola* to its bones, and were selling blubber and whale oil. Clark had neglected to bring much in the way of trading goodies. Even with her help, he only ended up with 300 pounds of blubber and a few gallons of oil. Sigh. Men.

During her twenty-one months (1804-1806) as an unpaid employee, Sacagawea went beyond her job description: she'd haggled for horses, she'd rescued equipment during storms, she'd even kept Lewis from a date with a tomahawk wielded by an angry chief. But the toughest part of the whole expedition was being the sole woman in a group of thirty-three men, most of them suffering from an indelicate disease called "syphilis". (And we thought it was the rain that made them crabby!)

Nevertheless, her high-mileage moccasins made the round trip. Post-expedition, the teenager walked with her son to see Captain Clark in St. Louis. Well aware of Sacagawea's slave-like existence with her husband, Clark offered the "solution" of adopting her boy. Thinking of her child's welfare, Sacagawea agreed.

Like Pocahontas, Sacagawea's years were few. Although some accounts argue that she lived much longer, she most probably died of a fever in 1812 at Fort Manuel in South Dakota.

THE NON-DISNEY "DUSKY PRINCESS"

Most films and books still insist that in 1608, a Powhatan Indian with the now-megafamous nickname of POCAHONTAS "saved" John Smith, leader of a shivering group of colonists at Jamestown, by throwing herself in harm's way just as her chieftain dad was about to quarter the man's cranium.

Anthropologists know better: the whole affair was probably an adoption ritual. Nearly all tribes had them. As an honor, or to replace a dead clan member, Indians took non-tribal folk (even palefaces) "captive", then had them undergo a symbolic death in order to be "reborn" as adoptive tribe members. Decades later, Smith wrote about his close call with the "savages", saying that Pocahontas' "compassionate pitifull heart" kept him from a skull-crushing.

After the ceremony, teen Pocahontas kept on doing good deeds, such as bringing food to the colonists. In 1613, the Jamestownians repaid her kindness by kidnapping her. How sweet — a paleface adoption. Wrong. The English feared an attack by her dad, chief Powhatan, so they lured the girl aboard a British ship — holding her for ransom for a year. When the Powhatan tribes of the Algonquin Nation refused to play or pay, the Brits sent 150 men to burn native houses.

The colonists finally let Pocahontas go — but not without fearsome torture: she was given religious instruction, baptized as "Rebecca", and forced to wear English clothing, including those dreadful undergarments.

At eighteen and barely out of lockup, Pocahontas had another run-in with an Englishman — John Rolfe asked for her hand. Hungry for more English copper, Dad overlooked the kidnapping and pushed hard for the alliance. She wed Rolfe on April 5, 1614.

The man who introduced tobacco cultivation in the colonies, Rolfe dreamed up a scheme to get greater fiscal support for Virginia Colony from the nicotine-despising royals. He and his "dusky princess" would go to England and schmooze the king and queen personally!

Pocahontas, who'd barely gotten out of labor with her son, Tom, wasn't that keen to travel. But in 1616, off they went, dressed to the nines. As Lady Rebecca, Pocahontas was presented at court and attended a performance of Shakespeare's *The Tempest*. The English loved her, they lionized her, they painted portraits of her wearing a stovepipe hat and a choky big ruff. She even had a string of "Beautiful Savage" taverns named in her honor.

In March 1617, the Rolfe family was set to return to America when Pocahontas fell ill — from smallpox, French pox, or just that foul English climate. She was buried at Gravesend — a woman who made history (or mythology) before she was twenty-one.

MOTHER AND DAUGHTER GEESE

Both the English and the French argue that Mother Goose — the person and the rhymes — are theirs. Nevertheless, the Yanks have a dandy candidate of their own: ELIZABETH FOSTER, who at age twenty-seven married Isaac Goose of Boston. This gander came with ten goslings from a previous marriage. Elizabeth took on the instant family — and began her own, producing six babies, four of whom lived past childhood.

In time, her own daughter ELIZABETH GOOSE married a printer named Tom Fleet, a creative lad who was also procreative. Eventually the thunder of tiny feet competed with the clatter of the printing press. Liz the younger would have gone bonkers if it hadn't been for her mom, whose babysitting talents included the ability to recite and sing thousands of nursery rhymes. Some of them supposedly got published by Tom Fleet in 1719 as *Mother Goose's Melodies* — ten years before any Mother Goose rhymes hit print in England.

CHAPTER
NINE

Celebrity Kin & Significantly Overlooked Others

SURVIVAL OF THE FATTEST

Spaniard ISABEL DE GUEVARA wanted to go far. Really far. Thus when her dad signed up in 1534 for the Conquistador Special "See South America! Exploit natives, grab territory!" cruise, she lobbied hard to be included. When she and Dad and a shipload of groaning souls, mostly male, arrived on the shores of what would become Argentina, she immediately saw that the expedition planning had been slapdash, to put it kindly.

As she recounted in letters that are still kicking around Spanish archives, "After arriving at Buenos Aires, twenty women among 1,500 men, we were without provisions. There was so much hunger that after three months, one thousand had died . . . The men were so thin that all of the work was left to the

266

women, from washing clothes to tending the sick, making meals with what little we had, cleaning, standing guard . . ."

One bright note: Isabel was awfully glad she hadn't worked herself down to a size twelve for the voyage. This conquistadoring thing made dieting a breeze. As she noted, "Because women can sustain ourselves with little to eat, we didn't fade into weakness like the men."

Thanks to the disastrous leadership of Pedro de Mendoza, the fort at Buenos Aires was soon abandoned. Isabel then joined a band of soldiers and civilians headed for Asunción, the capital of Paraguay. During that hideous 800-mile trip, there was ample time for Isabel to ask herself: "Why did I leave Spain? And where the heck is Paraguay?"

She made it, however — unlike most of the party. Her dad also went MIA, presumably swallowed up by the jungle or puréed by piranhas while exploring inland waterways.

Paraguay's capital was actually livable. Isable settled in, met a nice guy who'd survived the rigors of South America, and got married in 1542. The ink was barely dry on the thank-you notes when her new groom, Juan de Esquivel, lost his head in a political squabble.

Wisely, Isabel decided to stick to being a merry widow and get what was coming to her, exploitation-wise. It took forever. Isabel had to lobby, lobby, lobby, writing endless letters to Princess Juana, the head of the Council of the Indies, to get her reward. Finally, in 1556, a mere twenty-two years after she'd landed on this difficult continent, Isabel won a partition of land and a matching set of Indian laborers for her very own. Today she's remembered as one of the founders of Buenos Aires.

VOTED OUT BY A LANDSLIDE

BEATRIZ DE LA CUEVA was the first to admit it: She was grumpy when her sister Francisca bagged Pedro de Alvarado, the rough and red-headed Spanish general who'd conquered some place called "Guatemala" and brought back gunnysacks of gold. But there was a bright side — Francisca didn't last a year in the fever-ridden environs of Veracruz, Mexico, the Alvarados' first home.

Even after he popped the question to her, Bea had to wait ten years for Pedro to "pacify" Guatemala before she could join him. By 1537, the bride-to-be was on her way from Spain to the New World. After what happened to sis, she wasn't about to go economy class, either. She sailed with three ships crammed with finery, and took along twenty maids of honor as brides for some of the soldiers.

When they saw the uncouth characters waiting to greet them, many of the women said, "No way!" Too late: their tickets said, "One way". But Beatriz was happy, and, as she repeatedly said, that was what was important. She kept herself busy becoming the leading light of the community, while Pedro headed out on a manly quest to the Yucatan, where he was fatally sat on by a horse. Before he expired in June 1541, there was a bit of good news: Pedro did manage to bequeath his wealth and his governor's post to his wife.

269

In official grief mode, new governor Bea gave orders: Show some respect! Make this palace black, inside and out! (This wasn't easy, since the palace clung to the side of one of Guatemala's many steep volcanic peaks, and there were no paint stores on the continent as yet.) Soon, however, she moved on to pleasanter things — like pocket lining. For her first executive act, she made her brother lieutenant governor, then set about the critical business of amassing an insta-fortune.

Things went well for a whole twenty-four hours or so. The royal treasurer, however, still smarting from being passed over for governor, put together a plot to overthrow Bea. She got word of the conspiracy from her spies and sent a military death squad to clean up the conspirators. Then everybody went back to bed — only to be awakened after midnight on September 10 by an enormous seismic *burp*! from that darned volcano, looming 12,000 feet overhead. The quake broke the eastern wall of its crater, sending tons of rock and millions of gallons of icy water from the crater's lake to crash down on Bea's palace and the village just below it. Hundreds of people, Spaniards and Indians alike, including Bea, died that night.

In 1580, Beatriz's stepdaughter Leonor, one of the few highborn survivors, made a lovely gesture: she reunited her father Pedro and Bea. The first two governors of Guatemala still share a cozy king-sized burial plot, and will for all eternity — or until the next major volcanic eruption.

20/20, EVEN FROM HORSEBACK

She was called "a smart, witty, sensible woman of influence" by her contemporaries — some of 'em even men. A tireless educator, businesswoman, horsewoman, and traveler, Bostonian SARAH KEMPLE KNIGHT once made a five-month solo journey through the then-lonely country to New York, traveling via Rhode Island, New Haven, and Westchester County. (You think gridlock is rough now — try the idiots who were on what passed for roads in 1704). The newly widowed Knight left her sixteen-year-old daughter at home to mind things while she went to take care of a New York relative's estate. The journal she kept projects her adventuresome spirit, bursting with amusing anecdotes of the people she met and the hazards she encountered, from leaky canoes to unwanted bedroom companions.

When nearly forty, she opened a school in Boston and taught for the next decade. Two of her pupils went on to shine: religious reader Samuel Mather and that man for all seasons, Ben Franklin. When apple bribes from pupils got old, Knight plunged into farm management, real-estate dealings, and tavern owner-ship in New London, Connecticut.

Though she was noted for her ability to teach writing, it would be 1865 before her own writings saw print. But Mrs. Knight's astute remarks on things like

271

the prevalence of divorce — among whites and Native Americans alike — sound uncannily modern.

As she put it, "The Indians are easily divorced. Either male or female says, 'Stand away,' and the deed is done. And indeed these uncomely 'stand aways' are too much in vogue among the English in this indulgent colony, as their records plentifully prove . . ."

Historians have corroborated this trend, noting that newspapers of the 1700s were filled with items about the large number of men — and women — who ran away from mates and children.

SPREAD 'EM, BENEDICT!

When you ran a New York City boardinghouse in wartime, as Mr. Townsend did in 1779, you couldn't be too particular. Any number of British officers stayed there. One of the draws may have been his daughter SALLY TOWNSEND, whose looks and charm had lodger Lt. Colonel Simcoe writing bad poetry about her eyes. Sally used her baby blues to good advantage. As a spy for the Americans, she listened in on Brits lolling about the kitchen, who used a cupboard for message drops and pickups. When not making goo-goo eyes, Simcoe had a frequent visitor named John Anderson. Overhearing various remarks about ammo and West Point, Sally broke British secret agent Anderson's cover. With him, Americans got a stupendous two-for-one: his papers showed that West Point's commander, Benedict Arnold, was about to sell out to the British! Thus the biggest turn-coat in Revolutionary history, whose name is now a synonym for "traitor", was identified thanks solely to Sally. The only mystery: Where was *she* in your history books?

ONE OF WASHINGTON'S
SECRET WEAPONS

SARAH OSBORN BENJAMIN was only a private's wife. Wherever the Continental Army went — Baltimore to Valley Forge — unpaid camp follower Sarah followed. She nursed. She baked bread. She struggled to get the bloodstains out of uniforms. Although General George often grouched that women reduced his army's mobility, he couldn't have done without them.

During the American march to recapture Philadelphia and on to Yorktown, Sarah kept cooking. Washington happened to notice her carrying food to the trenches and asked, "Aren't you afraid of the cannonballs?" She replied, "It wouldn't do for the men to fight and starve too."

She also saw the war's final action at Yorktown, where the Americans dug in under heavy fire. Throughout the night, the drums beat without stopping. The next morning, Sarah learned that the British had surrendered.

Knowing that nothing gives a dogface a better appetite than victory, Sarah headed for the trenches with the vittles she'd prepared. From there, Mrs. Benjamin witnessed the surrender. So close was she that she saw tears roll down one British general's face.

Fifty years after the war, a now-widowed Sarah claimed her husband's pension, outlining his service to the country — a claim that was rightfully hers as well.

REVERED BY TOO FEW

Two years after Paul Revere's much-swooned-over midnight ride, a leggy sixteen-year-old from Fredericksburg, New York, rode her favorite horse, Star, to warn of another British approach. On *her* rain-soaked ride of April 26, 1777, SYBIL LUDINGTON galloped twice as far as Paul Revere, knocking on farmhouse doors along a forty-mile route. "Two thousand Redcoats are raiding Danbury — muster at Ludington's!" was her message. Although she roused a substantial number of volunteers, enemy troops managed to escape to their ships. Sybil's hometown was later renamed Ludingtonville in her honor.

There were revered deeds by other heroines on horseback, too, including twenty-two-year-old DEBORAH CHAMPION, who rode from her home in Connecticut for two days to reach George Washington with urgent dispatches from her region. She bluffed her way through enemy lines, later writing about her mission: "pulling my calash cap still further over my face, I went on with what boldness I could muster. Suddenly I was ordered to halt ... A soldier in a red coat proceeded to take me to headquarters, but I told him it was too early to wake the captain and to please let me pass for I had been sent in urgent haste to see a friend in need, which was true if ambiguous. To my joy, he let me go, saying, 'Well, you are only an old

276

woman anyway,' evidently as glad to get rid of me as I of him."

Unlike icon Paul Revere, who was captured by the Brits ten miles into his ride (Longfellow's poem forgot that little mishap), Sybil and Deborah both completed their missions.

A MINT OF FRANKLIN FEMALES

For brains, industry, and patriotism, Ben Franklin had serious competition in his own family — most of it female.

Youngest of Ben's siblings, JANE FRANKLIN MECOM nearly got lost in the seventeen-kid shuffle. Long-lived Jane bore nine children, most of whom died after begetting kids of their own, leaving her to raise her grandkids — and four of her great-grandkids as well! Ill-starred in business as in offspring, Jane tried but often failed to make ends meet with lodgers and a small shop. Her best friend and lifelong correspondent was brother Ben; to his credit, he helped Jane often during her difficult life — and saw to it that her last years were happy ones.

Ben's daughter SARAH FRANKLIN BACHE was a dedicated political activist. A fundraiser for the American cause, she joined others in buttonholing more than 1,600 donors to kick in money. By 1780, the Revolutionary Army had 2,005 new shirts made by Sarah and local Philly fillies.

Ben's sister-in-law, ANN SMITH FRANKLIN, was another standout. Married to Ben's brother James, Boston publisher of the *New England Courant*, she dutifully ran the presses after he died. After nearly two decades of putting ink on paper, Ann tried retiring. Her son, however, who'd apprenticed as a printer with Ben,

278

expired unexpectedly. Now both a newspaper publisher and the official printer for the colony of Rhode Island, Ann churned out periodicals, books, and almanacs. She called them "Poor Robin's Almanacs", using her husband's pen name. At sixty-eight, with what must have been gratitude, she went to her final retirement.

MAKING THE FUR FLY — AND PAY

When Sarah met Johnny on the streets of Baltimore in 1784, the circumstances were unromantic — young Sarah Todd was scrubbing the steps of the family boardinghouse when along came John Jacob Astor, selling cakes.

A year later, the two were married — but it took Sarah's $300 dowry to get them rolling. SARAH TODD ASTOR opened a music store (her brother-in-law made instruments) in the boardinghouse, while her new husband went off to the northern woods of Canada and upstate New York, to barter for furs with flannel and firewater.

Before long, Sarah's emporium became "Musical Instruments and Furs 'R' Us". Since Sarah had more talent for judging premium fur, John gave her the pick of his pelts. When she wasn't tending the store or one of her litter of eight kids, Mrs. Astor cleaned the critter hides, displaying them to advantage between the tubas and violins. The woodwinds were slow movers; not so the beaver skins. Pretty soon her sign read, "High-Class Pelts, Pianos & Piccolos".

J.J., meanwhile, was raking in the money in the fur trade. Quicker than a Silicon Valley startup, they became millionaires. Sarah's family connections helped Astor borrow money to expand their enterprises, and Sarah's insistence on attendance at social events and the "right" church allowed him to meet and mix with powerful people like Aaron Burr.

Now that they were in the chips, Sarah began charging her husband for the advice and professional judgment she'd been rendering for free. Need a shipment of pelts appraised? Should we get into Manhattan real estate? It was $500 an hour, and no bed-partner discounts, either.

Although a notorious life-long skinflint, John Jacob considered his wife's fees well worth it. She in turn donated the money to charity, it was said — and continued to be his redoubtable partner in all ways until her death in 1834.

PUBLISH, YES; EMANCIPATE, NO

"No bargain there," thought savvy shoppers at the slave sale in Boston when they saw a frail child stumble down the gangway. But tailor John Wheatley and his wife, SUSANNAH, snapped her up, naming her "Phillis". Soon afterward the family saw the seven-year-old trying to write the alphabet with charcoal. Daughter MARY WHEATLEY took it upon herself to tutor the child in grammar, history, Latin, and geography.

At nine, Phillis could read and write fluently. By fourteen, her intellectual and poetic talents shone beyond Boston. After her first poem was published in the Newport *Mercury*, everyone raved about the young poet. Even Benjamin Franklin was a fan. When the muse hit, Phillis was encouraged to drop her tasks, use local libraries, and write. She even became "family" enough to be baptized as PHILLIS WHEATLEY — a Wheatley who was still a slave, however.

At twenty, the young wunderkind fell ill. The Wheatleys brought in their own physician, who recommended sea air. Nothing too good for their human chattel — Phillis went by ship to London. By now, her book of poetry, published in 1773 with the patronage of a British countess, had made her famous in England. Before she even got off the ship, Phillis was a society darling. She stayed with her countess; she got a gift copy of *Paradise Lost* from the Lord Mayor; she was praised by influential people.

Life was rosy. Then word came that Mrs. Wheatley was shockingly ill. After just five weeks in London, poor Phillis felt honor-bound to return. Oh well, one good thing about the abortive stay — thanks to pressure from British admirers, the young black poet won her freedom.

Poetry being a poor source of revenue (especially since she apparently got no royalties), Phillis continued to live with the Wheatleys. Although accounts are contradictory, it seems she married a free black named John Peters, who was either a grocer or a lawyer, but not much of a provider. In addition to financial woes, neither marriage nor childbearing seemed to suit the health or creativity of the fragile poet; she died at age thirty-one. None of her three children survived.

Brief as her life was, many celebrated people had taken notice of Phillis. In 1775, she had sent George Washington a letter with a poem in his honor. He invited her to visit him at his Cambridge headquarters, and she did. It might just be one of history's coincidences, but after they met, Commander Washington reversed one of his policies. From then on, black men could serve in the Continental Army.

UNLIKELY INDEPENDENCE ENGINEER

Born in 1797 into the prolific Hapsburgs ("If you've got a kingdom, we'll marry it"), LEOPOLDINA looked every inch the part: blonde curls, fair skin, and a South America-sized Hapsburg lip. It wasn't easy being a multinational marriage pawn. Her sister Marie-Louise had returned quicker than a cheesy Christmas gift from her ill-fated coupling with a moody Bonaparte.

At nineteen, Leopoldina was picked to procreate with Pedro of Portugal, a spoiled looker with a taste for high living and low women. Pedro would rule Portugal's new prize, Brazil — with Leopoldina as empress.

The teen and her entourage took a year to reach Rio de Janeiro — just time enough for her to get fluent in Portuguese, her ninth language. In her luggage, this culture vulture had a huge library (librarian included) and a full orchestra to play hot Mozart tunes. A scientific sort, Leopoldina loved plants and bugs. How lucky — plenty of ghastly new samples where she was going.

Once in Brazil, between cycles of anesthetic-free childbearing and multiple miscarrying, Leopoldina wrestled with affairs of state — and just plain affairs. Not hers — Pedro's. Scandalmongers had plenty to monger about, including a carioca cutie named DOMITILA. Despite Pedro's sexual vagabonding,

Leopoldina tried to give her husband the backbone to endorse the independence movement, as she did, having seen how the tide was turning. Slow on the uptake, Pedro was pushed into exile. In his absence, the empress met with the council of state, declaring, "This country is now a Portugal-free zone!" This made her even more popular with the locals.

Too bad she couldn't win her own freedom. After Pedro slunk back to the capital, Leopoldina endured the fun of pregnancies in tandem with his very public mistress, who was lodged in a palace just spitting distance from her own digs. Well-loved but worn out, she died after giving birth to her ninth child. Dynastically speaking, though, she had the last guffaw: her son Pedro de Alcántara eventually became Brazil's "just for fun" figurehead ruler, Pedro II.

LOVE SLAVE — A WHOLE NEW MEANING

Two hundred years after her carnal caper with a U.S. president, SALLY HEMINGS has finally gotten satisfaction. Her long-term relationship with Thomas Jefferson, human rights booster and lifelong slaveholder, has been borne out by DNA testing of their descendants.

Born a slave in 1773, young Sally came to Monticello plantation the year after Tom Jefferson married MARTHA WAYLES. Although they weren't gift-wrapped, Sally and her mother Betty were wedding presents from the Wayleses. In sordid fact, Sally and several of her siblings had the same randy, equal-opportunity white father as Tom's new bride. That made Martha and Sally half-sisters — no wonder both women proved irresistible to Tom.

When "Dashing Sally" was in her early teens, she consoled lonely guy Jefferson, who by then was moping, wifeless, and forty-five, around the plantation. When Tom won the post of Ambassador to France, he asked Sally to bring over his younger daughter Polly. Besides getting to see the sights and suck up a few escargots, Sally lapped up some education — and the eye-opening notion of being a free woman, at least while in France.

Three years later, when Jefferson and Hemings returned to Virginia in 1789, they were an item. And more so, after Sally popped out a son, and then another, and so on, for a total of five or six children, some or all of them fathered by Thomas J, it's now believed.

Although he and Sally had a long-term intimacy, Jefferson was oh-so-conflicted about miscegenation — to say nothing of slavery itself. Here was a guy with vast landholdings, huge indebtedness (thanks to his incessant rebuilding of Monticello), and 200 slaves. He didn't hold with the mixing of the races, yet that was how he lived his life. He became famous for his writings on freedom; but in later life he advocated "diffusion", the quaint notion that allowing slavery to spread beyond the South was the best way to end it!

When tall, red-haired, light-eyed Jefferson died in 1826, there were dozens of tall, ruddy, light-complected slaves to mourn him. In life he had agonized over keeping his "slave family" intact. Nevertheless, Jefferson's debts were such that 130 humans were sold down the river after his funeral — including a couple of the Hemings clan. As if that weren't enough of a low blow, Sally didn't even get freed in Tom's will. She was eventually manumitted by one of Jefferson's white daughters. Surrounded by her descendants, the dashing one lived into her sixties.

WHY THE PREZ WAS PRO-EDUCATION

Even when her widowed daddy was in France during her school years, young PATSY JEFFERSON heard from him. A lot. Although Patsy adored poetry and an occasional trashy novel, the future president urged his eldest daughter to concentrate on French, drawing, dancing, music, and useful subjects like math.

His reasoning was interesting — and says a lot about what he thought of other males. "The chances are that in marriage, Patsy will draw a blockhead, I calculate at about fourteen to one," he wrote. With that in mind, he added, "So the education of her family will probably rest on her own ideas and direction without assistance."

Old Tom was right on target, sad to report. Patsy married a son of one Colonel Randolph, a lad with a terrific sperm count (the couple produced twelve offspring) but not much else to offer. During her marriage, Patsy managed the wobbly family finances because her husband was deeply in debt most of the time. And those were the good times. Her spouse also suffered from mental illness. When he took a break from sanity now and then, Patsy had to feed and educate the brood as best she could.

Patsy did get a little joy out of life, however. From 1801 on, during the two Jefferson administrations, she got to act as official hostess for her father, often hosting dinners and events at the President's Mansion. Thomas

Jefferson never remarried — although he dallied deeply with slave SALLY HEMINGS. Ironically, it was daughter Patsy who freed Sally after Jefferson's death. Looks like Daddy was pro-education for some women — and pro-shackles for others.

MORMON MAIDENHEADS — THEY'RE SPECIAL

Since 1827, EMMA SMITH had worked her tail off, helping her husband Joseph get his new Mormon religion rolling. The moving was a killer. She'd just gotten a decent household set up in New York, when — *boom!* — they had to move to Ohio. Then things got ugly, and it was good-bye Ohio, hello Missouri. Then Illinois.

Now Joe had the nerve to tell her that God had just sent him an urgent e-mail, saying there was a big problem with virgins. It seems that nobody with a maidenhead could enter Mormon heaven. "So, Emma dear, I've gotta make sure our virgins get through the Pearly Gates, don't I? So don't expect me for dinner next week, I'll be getting married a few more times . . ."

Then she found out that Mormon Number 1 had already prepped half a dozen virgins for halo status by secretly marrying them. After doing a slow burn, Emma played her trump card. She threatened to quit as Joe's full-time secretary and head of the Female Relief Society. "Dump those other wives, or else," she roared. Her husband countered with, "Two. How about just two?" On learning she'd be the only wife wearing an official Joseph Smith Mormon wedding ring, Emma grumpily caved in.

Little did she know that the Big Prevaricator immediately started refreshing his spousal stockpile in secret. In 1844, however, the disgruntled husband of a newly stockpiled wife exposed Joseph Smith and accused him in print of practicing "abominations and whoredoms". Thrown into jail, Smith was attacked by a lively mob. He jumped from his cell window; but by the time he hit the ground, the Mormon head of extracurricular activities was well ventilated with bullets.

The remaining Mormons immediately headed west. Emma, however, settled in Nauvoo, Indiana. Often heard to pooh-pooh Joseph's "revelations" about multiple marriage, she eventually wed a fellow who had no pesky Mormon leanings whatsoever.

Meanwhile, 2,000 miles to the west, ELIZA SNOW (one of Joseph's secret time-share brides) settled in Utah and became one of the wives of Brigham Young, the even more polygamous prophet who took Joseph's place. Eliza eventually won the nickname "the mother of Mormonism" — a claim that would have elicited a snort of derision from Emma Smith.

BEHIND BIG BIRD

Pop quiz for bird lovers: In the 435 avian portraits made by John James Audubon for his *Birds of America*, who painted the plants, flowers, insects, and other details? Answer: Unsung assistants, chiefly the modest MARIA MARTIN, a South Carolina artist.

From the age of thirty-one, Maria had lived with her ailing, perennially pregnant sister Harriet and Harriet's impregnator, a Lutheran minister named John Bachman. Single and well-fixed financially, Maria's goal was to make her sister's burden lighter.

Minister Bachman loved natural history; the household was filled with specimens of flora and fauna. Maria readily took to the frequent family field trips, where her talent for capturing plants and animals in accurate and beautiful ways soon became apparent.

In 1831, an already celebrated John James Audubon came to South Carolina. The delighted Bachmans pressed him to stay at their Charleston home. In no time, they'd ripped up the basement to make a studio, complete with all the freshly killed and stuffed birds he could ever want.

Seeing her work, the big bird-man asked Maria to paint a few feathered friends. He was so taken with the result that he hired her to do his backgrounds. It was a demanding job: the branches, flowers, and tiny creatures had to be as detailed as Audubon's, exactly to his scale, and just as magnificent.

Audubon was delighted. In a letter to Bachman, he wrote, "I much wish that your Dear Sister, our Sweetheart, would draw plants and branches of trees for me, about 15 or 20 drawings for small plates." He even named a hairy woodpecker subspecies for her — *Picus martinae*. All told, Maria painted thirty or more backgrounds; some scholars speculate that she painted some of the birds, too.

Maria played a big if invisible role in every one of Audubon's publications, painting and also editing (with John Bachman) the text for *Ornithological Biography* and *Viviparous Quadrupeds of North America*.

After Audubon and her cherished sister Harriet died, it wasn't a stretch to see that Maria and John Bachman would become mates. They got hitched in 1848. Throughout her long life, Maria continued painting. When her right arm gave her trouble, this serene problem-solver taught herself to draw left-handed — at age sixty!

THE BIG BANG

Brave new world, *c'est moi*, said MARIE-MADELEINE-SOPHIE ARMANT BLANCHARD, as she and a hot-air balloon headed skyward around 1800. Second wife of crotchety French balloonist Jean-Pierre Blanchard, who'd already flown many strange beasts of the air, Marie felt it was high time she got high. When she and the recent widower had met at his ascent in 1798, *l'amour* had struck. Eighteen-year-old Marie-Madeleine was dazzled by Jean-Pierre. OK, so her new mate had flopped in his recent try at conquering America by air, but with her at his side, they would conquer the world by basket.

On Marie's maiden flight, France was at her feet. Literally. This ballooning thing was fabulous. The only thing that got her aeronautical wicker in a twist was the thought of that hussy, MARIE ELIZABETH THIBLE, the French opera diva who'd had the honor of being the first woman aloft on a free flight. People were still gasping over the way she'd flown high over Lyons for forty-five minutes on June 4, 1784.

Still, the new Mrs. Blanchard was giving the lighter-than-air industry a little glamour. Her costumes! Her themed ascents! *Très magnifique!* Pretty soon La Blanchard had clocked dozens of events. She got terrific press from her 1810 Wedding Special ascent for the nuptials of Napoleon and Marie-Louise of Austria.

The royals ate it up — everyone except Josephine, who was still vexed over Bonaparte's "annulment" of their marriage.

Marie's sole problem: how to top her successes. In 1819, now a buxom thirty-nine and still looking good, Marie-Madeleine planned a pièce de résistance. Forget hot-air balloons — she was ready for some serious aeronautics: a hydrogen balloon ascent, framed by a thrilling fireworks display. On July 6, the balloon — and Marie — went up.

Jean-Pierre wasn't there to see it, having unluckily taken the fast lane in a parachute descent ten years earlier. Still, he would have tingled at the magnitude of Marie's show. Gorgeously costumed and waving the flag of France, she ascended to the heavens in a cockleshell like that of Botticelli's Venus.

At the peak of the action, however, the fireworks acted as a fuse for her flammable vehicle, setting off the most memorable fire and explosion France (and neighboring countries) had ever seen. Intrepid Marie became airborne in a way she hadn't planned on — and ballooning suffered its first female casualty.

Although it was fatal, Madame B's feat only fanned the flames of ballooning frenzy across the Atlantic. A mere six years later, the world would goggle at the first female Yank to soar solo.

THE *OTHER* UNDERGROUND RAILROAD

Always a limelight-shunner, homebody ANNA MURRAY DOUGLASS kept a low profile while her worthy husband Frederick got all the glory. But Fred wouldn't have become who he was without Anna.

She was the first child among the Murrays to be born free. At seventeen, she left home to do maid's work for a French family in Baltimore, where she met — and fell in love with — a clever and eloquent guy named Fred Bailey. Slight hitch to getting hitched: her boyfriend was a slave.

For Anna, the path to true love required major problem solving. Item 1: They had to engineer his escape. Generous Anna forked over nine years' savings to Freddie — and those servant-sized pittances added up. She even sold her feather bed for extra cash.

Instead of making herself a wedding gown, she sewed Bailey a sailor-suit disguise. Then she forked out more cash for some fake papers at the nearest "Runaway Bogus Docs While-U-Wait". In 1838, all was ready. Fred fled Baltimore for New York, where he rendezvoused with Anna. Wedding bells at last! To cover their tracks, the couple immediately moved to Bedford, Massachusetts, changing their last name to Douglass.

There, Anna plugged away as a domestic, while Fred worked at crummy grunt-labor jobs. Both moonlighted as social activists. Pretty soon Fred was getting lots of calls to travel and speak for the abolitionist movement; unfortunately, few were paid engagements. Anna, who by that time had five children underfoot, again took up the financial slack. She assembled shoes and cleaned houses while Douglass continued to organize people in the United States and England and to publish his abolitionist newspaper.

In 1847, the Douglasses moved to Rochester, New York. As if keeping food on the table and raising the kids single-handedly weren't enough, Anna took on another job. From her modest home, an Underground Railroad stop for slaves fleeing the South, she acted as agent whenever her husband was absent. That worked out to be most of the time. (This would be three years before Harriet Tubman began helping slaves to escape the South.)

Sad to relate, in the later years of the Douglass marriage, Freddy became an international celebrity — a man who liked to be seen with other women (black and white) — and a snob. Like a plastic surgeon who's been put through med school on the secretarial wages of his wife, Douglass got sniffy about Anna's lack of education — and conveniently myopic about her king-sized contributions, financial and otherwise. When Anna died after a long illness, Frederick pulled out all the clichés and wed a young, white, trophy college grad who'd been his secretary.

For Uppity Women Who Want to Get Into the Act

New World Resources

To learn more about the women in this book and other formidable females from history, join one of these organizations. Go online to female-friendly sites. Visit these unusual museums and historic landmarks. Take part in Living History events and celebrations like the Lewis and Clark Bicentennial. Sample life as it was lived, at faithful replicas from Williamsburg to Native American villages.

ORGANIZATIONS

- **American Association of University Women** (AAUW), 1111 16th Street NW, Washington, DC 20036. Library, archives, and funding sources for grants and fellowships.

- **Bethune Museum and Archives for Black Women's History**, 1318 Vermont Avenue NW, Washington DC 20005; (202) 332-1233.

- **Black Women's Educational Alliance**, 6625 Greene Street, Philadelphia, PA 19119.

- **National Coordinating Committee for the Promotion of History**, 400 A Street SE, Washington, DC 20003. Advocates for representation of women in the National Park Service's Historic Landmark program, among other activities.

- **National Museum of Women in the Arts**, 1250 New York Avenue NW, Washington, DC 20005-3920. Has holdings of numerous female artists from the past and present. Activities include exhibits, seminars, and a beautiful quarterly publication with membership.

- **National Women's History Project**, 3343 Industrial Dr., Suite 4, Santa Rosa, CA 95403; (707) 636-2888. Wonderful umbrella organization for women's history archives, annual events, teacher workshops, books, and much more.

- **Women Count**, Public Media Center, 466 Green Street, Suite 300, San Francisco, CA 94133; (415) 522-9902. A nonpartisan group.

- **Women of All Red Nations**, 4511 North Hermitage, Chicago, IL 60640. Information on Native American women.

PUBLICATIONS AND ONLINE RESOURCES

- Connect with one of the many chapters of the Lewis and Clark Trail Heritage Foundation at *www.lewisandclark.org*.

- *Living History* magazine, P. O. Box 77, Fairfax, VA 22030; (703) 758-5838.

- For Mayflower genealogy, online at: *http://members.aol.com/calebj/mayflower.html*.

- Go to *www.nwhp.org*, the National Women's History Project Web site, to get their excellent catalog and other materials.

- *No Quarter Given Pirate Newsletter*, P. O. Box 7456, Riverside, CA 92513-7456, (909) 785-1233.

- *The Pine Tree Shilling* quarterly, P. O. Box 1005, Charleston, NH 03603.

- *Susan B. Anthony Slept Here*. Sherr, Lynn, and Jurate Kazickas. New York: Times Books, 1994. A huge and inexpensive reference standout, bursting with photos, directions to landmarks, and stories about many of the women in the book you hold.

- *Smoke and Fire News*, a monthly newspaper with detailed listings of Living History events in the United States and Canada, including Native American powwows, Revolutionary War-era events, and other history buff get-togethers. P. O. Box 166, Grand Rapids, OH 43522; (419) 832-0303. Or get eighteenth-century goods and history books from the Smoke and Fire Company, 27 North River Road, Waterville, OH 43566.

- Check out the women's online networks iVillage, Oxygen, and *femina-cybergrrl.com*, called "the Yahoo of women's links".

- You may also want to investigate online magazines *moxie.com* and *workingwoman.com*, both of which appear in print format as well.

PLACES TO VISIT, EVENTS TO SEE

- The only primary source documents for Sacagawea are the journals of Lewis and Clark; the best collection is at the **American Philosophical Society** in Philadelphia, Pennsylvania.

- **Colonial Williamsburg** (the second colonial capital of Virginia), **Jamestown** (the first permanent English settlement in America), and **Yorktown** (site of a key victory in the Revolutionary War), easy driving distance of one another, form the Historic Triangle. The village of Williamsburg glories on 500 buildings on 173 acres, 100 restored, the others reconstructed, where interpreters in period dress put on programs. Jamestown settlement has a Powhatan Indian village, ship replicas, and a fort with folk in period dress. Yorktown has a visitors' center, museum, and a self-guided auto tour of points of interest.

- **Prudence Crandall Museum**, P. O. Box 47, Routes 14 and 169, Canterbury, CT 05331; (203) 546-9916. Exhibits, museum at the first school for young black women in New England.

- **Nancy Hart State Park** in northeast Georgia has a replica of her cabin on it. Near Elberton, on Hart Highway in Hart County.

- Board the *Mayflower II*, a replica of the original, near Plymouth Rock at the harbor in Plymouth, Massachusetts.

- "Old Glory", Mary Pickersgill's handiwork, is on display at the **National Museum of American History,** one of fourteen museums of the Smithsonian Institution, located on the Mall, Washington, DC.

- **The Star-Spangled Banner Flag House,** 844 East Pratt Street, Baltimore, MD; (410) 837-1793. Now a National Historic Landmark, this was the home of Mary Young Pickersgill, creator of "Old Glory".

- **National Women's Hall of Fame,** 76 Fall Street, Seneca Falls, NY 13148; (315) 568-2936. Gallery, educational programs.

- In **New Orleans,** visit Jackson Square, partly built by Micaela Almonaster; see the Ursuline convent where Henriette DeLille worked; and get a cheap thrill at the tomb of voodoo queen Marie Laveau at St. Louis Number 1 Cemetery on Basin Street, followed by a stop at the Historical Voodoo Museum on nearby Dumaine Street.

- **Oconaluftee Indian Village** in Cherokee, North Carolina (near the Great Smoky Mountains National Park) recreates a circa-1750s Cherokee village, with Native Americans in period dress, plying traditional crafts from canoe carving to basket making.

- Visit **Plimouth Plantation** (two miles from Plymouth Rock on South Route 3A), a replica of the original Pilgrim village of 1627, plus the Wampanoag Summer settlement, staffed by native Americans. Both with period dress, activities.

- **Pocahontas State Park,** in Chesterfield, VA, thirty miles from Richmond.

- Pocahontas is the centerpiece of the **Powhatan Renape Nation's American Indian Heritage Museum,** P. O. Box 225, Rancocaa, New Jersey 08073; (609) 261-4747. Also see a traditional woodland village, buffalo, and nature trails on the reservation. The Powhatan Renape Nation has its own Web site, which can be accessed using the key word *Pocahontas*.

- **Betsy Ross House,** her 1740s home and workshop; she's buried in the courtyard. 239 Arch Street, Philadelphia, PA.

- To honor the memory of accused witch Grace Sherwood, visit **Witch Duck Point,** on the Lynnhaven River near Virginia Beach, VA.

- **The Women's Memorial,** 5510 Columbia Pike, Suite 302, Arlington, VA 22204-3123. Honors 2 million women who've served in the U.S. military; also has a permanent database. Administered by the Women in Military Service for America Memorial Foundation (WIMSA), Dept. 560, Washington, DC 20042-0560.

- Check the listings throughout the year (more in good-weather months) in the *Smoke and Fire News* and other publications. Typical offerings: the History Fair in Kalamazoo, MI, each fall; the annual fair at New Boston, a reenactment of a 1790-1810 trade fair, held near Springfield, Ohio; Alabama Frontier

Days, held in Wetumpka, Alabama, in November; the annual Children's Powwow, sponsored by the Santa Fe Indian School in Santa Fe, New Mexico.

- At "witch hunt central", in Salem, Massachusetts, you'll get insights at the **Witch House** (actually the home of the judge who presided in 1692), at 310½ Essex Street; (617) 744-0180.

- Much more moving is the **Witchcraft Victims' Memorial** site at 176 Hobart Street in nearby Danvers (the original Salem Village).

- **Fort Clatsop National Memorial,** near Astoria, Oregon, is one of five national event sites for the Lewis & Clark Bicentennial; in a woodland setting, an excellent reconstruction of the winter quarters where Sacajawea and company spent much of 1805-06. Find them online at *nps.gov/focl*.

Index

As you'll see, uppity women of this era went through husbands, surnames, and nicknames like you wouldn't believe. In this book, within each entry, only the name or names by which a woman was most commonly known are given. In this index, however, all the monikers for each woman are listed.

Another thing you'll notice: over time, first names were "mplaced". Thus some women are known only by surname, and are indexed under "madame", "miss", "mistress", or even "widow".

As in the previous books in the series, the index is organized by first name rather than surname(s), if any. This is done largely to protect the author's sanity.

In Gratitude

A rousing *Thank you!* to all the folks who gave of their time and knowledge to make this book a better one; and a special helping of gratitude to the following:

Reference librarian Mary Ann Shaffer, and Inter-Library Loans staff Diane Loomis and Lisa Moon, at the Olympia Service Center.

Intrepid librarians Iver Matheson, Billy Bob Tubbs, Michelle Zilli, Fred Mattfield, and Sue Cowell at the Ocean Park Timberland Library.

The helpful staff at the Women's Memorial, including curator Judith Bellafaire, Britta Granrud, and the memorial's founder, Brig. General Wilma Vaught, USAF (ret.).

The clues, encouragement, and leads from Trish Jamison Graboske; Blue Magruder; Charlotte Anderson; Clark Harris McClaskey; Rex DesBrisay; and Robin Maxwell.

And the extra-uppity contributions of Major Bonnie O'Leary, USAF (ret.); author Tom Ogren; researcher Margot Kellysmyth Kellam; and the eternally awesome Stan Thompson.